From
FBI AGENT
TO AN
APOSTLE

Saga of a Spiritual Sniper

By Frank Burton, Jr.

ACKNOWLEDGEMENTS

⎯⎯∾∾∾⎯⎯

I want to first thank God who is my everything! He is truly YAHWEH to me. God has kept me safe and has allowed me to navigate a 22 ½ year career as a FBI Special Agent. The Lord kept me free from all hurt, harm and danger during this time. He has guided, guarded and governed me as I have traveled this wonderful, rewarding and at times – very dangerous career. Despite colleagues being shot and killed in the line of duty and working dangerous undercover assignments in some of this Country's most dangerous cities, God allowed me to come through it all unscathed. It is this same God who has called me to the ministry of the Gospel of Jesus Christ. He has called me to serve as an Apostle. Thank You God!

To my lovely and awesome wife Tasey Burton! Without you, none of this would have ever been possible. We have always approached things together: —-shoulder-to-shoulder, back-to-back and face-to-face. You have been my number one cheerleader for twenty-five years. You encouraged me when I was going through the FBI application process and you cheered me on as I finally answered the call of God on my life to preach the Good News of the Gospel of Jesus Christ. You have been the love of my life, my confidant and best friend. All the while, you have also been my co-laborer in Christ (Pastor and Co-Founder of Perfect Will Ministries). Tasey, words on these pages will never be able to adequately express the depth of my love for you, so I'll just say thank you and I love you very much.

To my wonderfully blessed children: Christopher, Arielle, Frank III, and Zach... GREATNESS IS IN YOU! I see so much potential in you all and pray that you continue to strive for God's best and highest will in your lives. You make me proud to be your Dad!

To Frank Sr. and Florence Burton (Mom and Dad), you are responsible in a large part of the man I have become. Your example and influence have assisted me to get to where I am today. I love you, as well and say, thank you!

To my only sibling, Belinda M. Rhinehart. Wow, so many childhood memories have carried me to this point. May God continue to richly bless you and the Rhinehart family.

To Curtis Hairston, I thank God for our ordained encounter. What a wonderful kinship that has developed over the past seven years. Thanks for giving me the opportunity to truly serve the body of Christ's most and prolific ministers. I am encouraged and inspired at how you stepped out on faith and authored your first book: "Who Is Watching While They Pray?" Thanks Curtis!

Apostle Kimberly and Apostle Ardell Daniels, when God sent me on assignment with the FBI in the summer of 2004 to Jacksonville, FL, it was a God ordained assignment. The lessons-learned and hands-on spiritual warfare experience gained was been invaluable. I will go in greater detail in the next chapter, "Infectious Encounter." Thank you for your powerful ministry, it has had a serious impact on what we do at Perfect Will Ministries.

Bishop T.D. Jakes, Kirk Franklin, and Martha Munizzi, thank you for allowing me to serve you in your ministry efforts. Thank you for trusting the God in me and my ability to protect you. It has been both an honor and pleasure to serve. Dan and Martha , thank you for going that "extra mile" in the friendship that has developed between us as a result of our desires to please and serve God with excellence.

To my Bishop, Rev. Dr. C. Matthew Hudson, Jr. You walked into my life fourteen years ago and my life literally changed in the blinking of an eye. Your presence, anointing, professionalism, guidance and influence is a huge portion of who I have become in the Lord. It was you who named the gifting and calling on my life. It was you who first uttered the words: "He is an Apostle!" I am proud to call you my Pastor, Covering and my Friend. Thanks for vision casting for me. I have sought to follow your example of excellence in much of what I have done in ministry. Mere words are not adequate to pay homage to you for all you have done for me. I'll just say, thanks!

Finally, to my Perfect Will Ministries Family. I have always said that Pastor Tasey and I have the BEST CONGREGATION IN THE WORLD! "We are contemporary but not compromised. We envision and experience a diverse, multi-cultural worshipping community of spiritually mature believers, leading others into a personal relationship with Jesus Christ. Producing healthy families, engaged in holistic ministries to develop the community, spiritually and economically impacting the World for the glory of God." PWM, remember what I've always told you: "WBTBU for the Kingdom of God..." so get ready!

PREFACE

First and foremost, please understand that I am just an ordinary person who has had some "extra ordinary" opportunities. I have had an extraordinary career, extraordinary call to ministry (a Theophany experience which I will explain later), extraordinary life experiences and am living out an extraordinary vocation. In this book I will detail the very fine line of being a Special Agent of the Federal Bureau of Investigation (FBI) and an Apostle. I will lay out the challenges and victories and how they intertwine, contrary to what many would imagine.

Each chapter is to challenge you to be the best you can possibly be in God. Moreover, I need you to get this in your spirit: "GREATNESS IS IN YOU!" I fully understand that One's story can have a powerful impact on another's life, even if it is just a small part of the story. No big words; no extravagant language; no hidden codes... just straight talk and to the point. Enjoy!

INTRODUCTION

⚯

Ever since I was a young boy, I was always charismatic. I could make people laugh when they were sad. I would have older folk (much older than myself) come for advice on various topics. I was a great listener and gave pertinent advice, even at such a young age. I was always a leader and as I grew older, I would become more and more accomplished. Now that I'm reflecting on this, there is a bible passage that says: "A man's gift makes rooms for him, and brings him before great men." (Proverbs 18:16 NKJV)

As the years went by, I would become a three-sport star in High School (making various All-State Teams and playing in Statewide All-Star Games). I was blessed to earn and receive a full four-year athletic scholarship to College for Football and because of my athletic ability; my College Football Coach would allow me to participate on the College's Baseball team. By the end of my College career I would go to Letter in Football and Baseball. As a member of the Baseball Team I was selected as Team Captain and in 1984 I would finish 9th in the Nation in Stolen Bases in NCAA – Division I Baseball for Delaware State College (now Delaware State University). I would graduate with a Bachelor's Degree in English in four years (1 of only 2 of my 30 classmates who earned Football Scholarships) and finish with a 3.25 GPA. In 2000, I was inducted into the Delaware State University's Athletic Hall of Fame for Football and Baseball. God has truly blessed me in this area of my life.

After College, I would work in at 1st National Bank of Wilmington; Glen Mills Schools as Counselor/Teacher; and then become a Special Agent with the FBI. I would have tremendous success as a FBI Agent and receive Commendations from FBI Directors Louis J. Freeh and Robert S. Mueller for cases I worked. Finally, I would answer my "Call" to the ministry and be ordained as an Apostle of the Gospel of Jesus Christ.

FORWARDS FOR FROM FBI AGENT TO AN APOSTLE

———⟨∾∿∾⟩———

"Working as a Pastor, Deacon, Apostle or other Godly position is a unique appointed calling from God. Apostle Burton recognized this calling sent directly from the Holy Throne Room.

Working for the FBI is also a special calling. Those chosen by God to join the FBI do so taking a personal commitment to serve others, protecting the Nation placing others before themselves.

I was blessed to work with Apostle Burton throughout his FBI Career. I recall sharing with Apostle Burton the direction I received from God that we had a mandate to hire God-fearing people into the FBI because the demonic forces of evil could not be overcome with merely a badge and a gun. The FBI needed God-Fearing people inclusive if persons from all walks of life.

Apostle Burton validated this ordained direction as he shared that many of his FBI successes with criminals were accomplished not with the Badge and the Gun but truly with the God-given Holy Armor of Spiritual Ware Fare!

I have personally witnessed Apostle Burton grow by leaps and bounds in his special calling serving in God's Army!!!

He has a pure, giving, kind heart and His Godly teachings are too powerful for earthly words! Being the daughter of a Pentecostal Minister, and living every day to serve ALL God's people, it was extremely easy for me to see the gift of Pastoring on him from the first day we met.

I am honored to call Apostle Burton a true friend and HIGHLY Anointed General in God's Army!

Congratulations Apostle Frank Burton, this book will enlighten our Global World for generations.

May God bless you today, tomorrow and beyond infinity."

Gwendolyn Hubbard
Executive Director, RTPC Sarel (Spain, Mauritania, Morocco, USA)

"Apostle Burton's book, 'From FBI Agent to an Apostle' was an inevitable writing. There are not many of us who are able to balance the 'Call' of God on our lives, with our God-given gift and duty of protecting others. Apostle Burton is that 'poster child'. In the past seven years or so, he has assisted me with a couple of my Principals on different occasions. Because of his professionalism, attention to detail and overall dedication to his 'Call', I continue to reach out to him for assistance. My Principal and I know we are always covered on the East Coast, first by our God, secondly by Frank Burton operating in the spirit of excellence.

When I wrote the book, 'Who Is Watching While They Pray?', I wrote it with men like me, Apostle Burton and others in mind. I wrote it thinking of the type of man who would lay down his life for his brother...for the sake of the "Call".

Curtis Hairston
Hairston Global Protective Services, Inc.
Dallas, TX

Fidelity. Bravery. Integrity.

Imagine what it's like to track down a drug lord. To capture a kidnapper. To break up a major crime family. To outsmart a computer whiz embezzling millions of dollars. These are the kinds of investigations FBI Special Agents perform every day.

Do you want to pursue an unparalleled opportunity to advance in your career? As a Special Agent with the FBI, you'll have every opportunity to rise in the ranks and lead others in a supervisory role.

Accomplishment? FBI Special Agents accomplish more in one year than most people do in an entire career. The service they perform for their country and their community bring a satisfaction few other jobs can match. In addition,

FBI Special Agents earn an excellent salary, benefits and retirement package.

Are you interested in a career with the FBI? Right now, we're looking for men and women, across the country, to become FBI Special Agents. Among the basic qualifications: a college degree, availability for assignment anywhere in the Bureau's jurisdiction, must be at least 23 years of age and not more than 36, and be in excellent physical condition. If you're interested in working for the world's most sophisticated law enforcement agency, contact your local FBI office. An equal opportunity employer.

Special People. Special Agents.

1

INFECTIOUS ENCOUNTERS

"When Faith replaces Fear… then success will replace Failure."

There are no "chance" meetings or "chance" encounters in God! There are no coincidences, nor are there any "OMG" connections, because He is God! He knows all things and does everything well.

Every relationship we develop and/or experience whether it is good or bad… is intentional! God does things on purpose and for purpose. Every encounter therefore, is purposeful. If it is an encounter that is not to our liking, we must remember that God is not a "child abuser" and no matter what the extent of your hurt or discomfort, His goal is never intended to harm you. With that, I might offer this bit of advice to you: Don't ever mistake God's process for punishment. Sometimes we have to endure e "valley experiences" in order to appreciate our "mountain top" experiences. Remember, it is virtually impossible for you to go from mountain top to mountain top without first coming down and traveling through the valley. So embrace your "valley experience" and learn all that God has in store for you while you are there.

So we must be "Intentional" in our encounters! We must "INFECT" every single encounter with the love, spirit, presence and the very essence of the Holy Spirit. To take a term from my accomplished sports past (and I know this to be true in many areas of life): "You only get ONE time to make a best and lasting First impression." This was a motto I lived by when competing in sports camps and showcases. On those particular days you had to demonstrate your best! For many, there were no "second chances" or "do overs." You had to be on your "A" game at that very moment. You had to bring it! No excuses!

Some of the Intentional and Infectious Encounters in my life that have "born much fruit" and have endured the test of time include:

My Wife; Dr. C. Matthew Hudson, Jr (My Pastor and Covering); Curtis Hairston (Bishop T.D. Jakes ministries); Sean Smith (Bishop T.D. Jakes ministries); Bishop T.D. Jakes (Bishop of the Potter's House – Dallas, TX); Apostle Kimberly Daniels (Pastor and Founder of Spoken Word Ministries in Jacksonville, FL, Kimberly Daniels Ministries International, and the Word Bible College) and her husband Apostle Ardell Daniels (affectionately known as Apostle "Danny"); Kirk Franklin (Gospel Musician, Choir Director, Radio & TV Host, Award Nominated and Winner for Gospel Music); Bazi Kanani (correspondent for ABC News, assignments included Nairobi, Kenya. Presently in the Washington, D.C. area); Maurette Brown Clark (Multi Stellar Award Winner, Dove Nominated, Gospel Recording Artist) and her husband Mark; Martha Munizzi (Internationally acclaimed and award nominated and winning Gospel Recording Artist – Dove, Stellar, Oasis, Christian Music Awards, & CCM Magazine's Reader Choice) and her husband Dan; Tug McGraw (MLB Relief Pitcher & Sports Caster, also father of Country Music Artist – Tim McGraw)Tony Graffanino (MLB Player); Tom McGlawn (MLB Player); Kerry Fraser (Retired NHL Referee & Future Hall of Famer); Roy Williams (NFL Dallas Cowboys); Rick Williams (6 ABC News Anchor-Philadelphia); Nefertiti Jaquez (NBC 10 Reporter – Philadelphia); Father Mike Mannion (FBI EAP Chaplain & Priest who worked with Mother Teresa); Picc Samuels (FBI EAP Coordinator); and Pastors Eddie and Dana Rivas (Newark, NJ). Pastor Eddie encouraged me with these words: "You are not in the business of building Mega Churches, but God sent you to build MEGA PEOPLE." I take that assignment seriously. Thanks Pastor!

I won't list or them all, but will give examples of how a few of these "infectious encounters" developed. On Wednesday, September 1, 2004 while on assignment with the FBI in Jacksonville, FL, I had the pleasure of meeting Apostle Kimberly Daniels and her awesome husband, Apostle "Danny." Apostle Alexander Thompson who sat on my ordination council insisted that I connect with these two "powerhouses!" So, while working a terrorist related matter, I attended their bible study at Spoken Word Ministries (Steele St. and Blue Ave.). After bible study, Apostle Kim gave me some spiritual warfare tapes to listen to and Apostle Danny invited me to connect with him on the next day.

On Wednesday, September 5, 2001 while enjoying an Eastern Caribbean Cruise with my wife and I met Gospel Award winning singer Maurette Brown-Clark and her husband Mark. This was on the Fun Ship "Paradise." Before I really knew who Maurette was, I had befriended her and Mark. Ironically, I had a very good childhood friend (Tia Thompson) who was a longtime entertainer on Carnival Cruise lines. Only God worked this out that

Miss Maurette was one of the lead entertainers on our cruise. On that evening I introduced my new friends Mark and Maurette (along with others) to my old friend Tia. Tia took us on the behind the scenes tour of the ship, which was phenomenal. On the next evening, Maurette performed a Gospel Concert in the Queen Mary Lounge. The venue was packed and her ministry was anointed, so much so, that my wife was filled. Also, performing was Chris Byrd, who is a lasting friend of mine.

Our cruise made stops in Nassau, Bahamas, San Juan, Puerto Rico and St. Thomas. On Saturday, September 8th, my wife and I spent significant time with Maurette and Mark. Chris and his wife Bridgette also accompany us. I learned that Mark and Maurette lived in close proximity to us, so I told them that if I ever worked in their area I would stop by. We exchanged contact information and on Sunday, September 9, 2001, we returned home safely. Thank You Lord! We had no idea what would occur in the following two days.

One Tuesday, September 11, 2001, I returned back to work. While out on the Street working an Organized Crime figure, at 8:46 am, Flight 11 crashed into the north face of the North Tower of the World Trade Center, New York, New York. And at 9:03 am, Flight 175 crashed into the South Tower. Immediately, we were directed to go home and pack our bags. We would be re-directed to work at "Ground Zero." When I arrived home my parents were there and my children had been sent home from school. As I walked in I looked at my wife and the faces of my entire family. They knew! They knew I would have to leave and nobody knew when I was coming back. I'll talk about those details a bit later. What a tragedy!

While on assignment working the "Lackawanna 5," major World Terrorist from Yemen. I met Bazi Kanani. On Saturday, September 7, 2002, I met Bazi at the Barnes and Noble Book Store at 1565 Niagara Falls Blvd, Amherst NY (Romney Dr. and Niagara Falls Blvd). This was just outside of Buffalo, NY. Bazi was an anchor woman for WGRZ News 2, which was an NBC affiliate. Bazi looked sad, so I approached her and began to minister to her and encourage her. I told her that I was a minister and spoke life into her and encouraged her in the Lord. We exchanged contact information and I would occasionally reach out for her to see how she was doing. Bazi later returned to her home town of Denver, CO (working for KUSA-TV, Channel 9 News, NBC), where she was much happier. Eventually, God blessed Bazi to be able to work in the homeland of her father. She was promoted to be a correspondent for ABC News and was assigned to Nairobi, Kenya where she reported on news from Africa, via ABC News broadcast, radio and website platforms. Today, Bazi has returned "State-Side," living in the Washington, D.C. area. She continues to work for ABC as a correspondent and can be seen often on ABC's Good Morning America. On September 14, 2002 the "Lackawanna 5" were arrested in Lackawanna, NY. Our team was instrumental in the arrest of these World terrorist.

As I mentioned earlier, on September 1, 2004, I met Apostle Danny and his two wonder twins (Elijah and Elisha) at a Restaurant where we exchanged testimonies. Because my passion was Men's Ministry, Apostle Danny gave me an opportunity to minister to the men of Spoken Word Ministries on Saturday, September 4, 2004. What a powerful study! We began to cast out demons which manifested in several men who attended the fellowship. Apostle Danny is such a powerful man of God when it comes to deliverance ministry. While in Jacksonville I found myself directly in the middle of Hurricane Frances. I made calls back to Philadelphia Headquarters anticipating the hurricane and attempted to have our troops return to Philadelphia, but our instructions where to "bunker in." This hurricane was forecasted as a Category 4 storm with sustained winds of 145 mph. All of Jacksonville was in an uproar.

Apostle Kim called for the Church members and anyone else who would pray to come out and pray that it would not be as bad as forecasted. We prayed on Saturday night and then again during Sunday morning worship Service. We prayed that God would intervene and because the prayers of the Saints, God would respond. On Sunday, September 5th, Hurricane Frances hit the State of Florida. Instead of a Category 4, it was downgraded to a Category 1 storm. Jacksonville had 80 mph sustained winds and experienced $10 million worth of property damage. Hurricane Frances was the size of the State of Texas and covered the entire State of Florida. People of God, can I just tell you that "God Turned It!" He turned it because of the remnant who prayed! Totally off topic, I had the chance to dine at CLARK'S FISH CAMP SEAFOOD RESTAURANT. This was a small restaurant located at 12903 Hood Landing Road, off of Julington River and near Old Bull Bay. Please don't ask me why, because I'm not normally like this, but I tried some of the crazy appetizers they offered. Menu items were labeled: "Call of the Wild Appetizers," to include: Fried Gator Tail, Charred Gator Sausage, Smoked Eel, Fried Turtle, Charred/Fried Rabbit, Charred Frog Legs, Charred Quail, Charred Ostrich, Charred Kangaroo, Charred Venison, Charred Buffalo, Charred Antelope, and Charred Rattlesnake. Yuck! Again, I only braved a few of these items. To date, Apostle Danny and I have a formidable relationship and continue to encourage each other in the Lord.

I know that I'm jumping around a bit, but remember... I'm emphasizing how "Infectious Encounters" work. So stay with me through this passage. I promise you that it will all tie together.

Being "Law-Enforcement" minded and very watchful, I believed it prudent to take a selected group of Perfect Will Ministries members with me to Dallas, TX, to attend the S.T.O.P.P.E.D. training. This was Church Security Training to make Church's more aware of incidents that occur or could possible occur to disrupt or disquiet a Church service. It equipped each team for being capable of adequately addressing such incidents. The Conference was from March 1st to March 3rd of 2007. After completing one of the scenarios, Sean Smith, of the Potter's House and organizer of the Training, pulled me to the side and advised that I had to be in law enforcement or the military by the way I addressed the scenario's challenges. I never said a word about what my job was. I simply told him that I was an Apostle and Pastored a Church in DE.

Almost one month later, while working a Recruitment Career Fair at Lincoln University in Lincoln, PA, I got a call from Gwen Hubbard from the FBI's Human Resources Department. Gwen had strategically put together a National Recruitment Team (NRT). She advised me that our NRT would be headed to Dallas, TX to be sponsors at Bishop T.D. Jake's FOR MEN ONLY CONFERENCE. Excuse me? Say what? FBI setting up a booth to recruit at a Bishop T.D. Jakes venue? Are you serious?

We arrived and set up our FBI booth at the Conference on Thursday, March 29, 2007. Not a pretty site! We received several not so kind comments and people questioned what the FBI was doing at this event. As people walked by during our setup period, they smirked at our posters and table coverings.

When the Conference opened up, our Team greeted each person in a professional and kind manner. The Team consisted of Unit Chief, Gwen Hubbard, Alicia Devina, Erin Badsen, James Atkinson, Manny Kindle, and myself. Each of us had outstanding interpersonal skills and was adept to dealing with people who responded adversely to the FBI. One by one, each person who stopped by our table realized that we were just normal people like them. We had normal lives, families and activities that we enjoyed, similar to them. We began to describe the opportunities the FBI presented for Special Agents, as well as, Professional Support personnel.

Here is the part nobody knew about! On Wednesday, March 28th, after arriving and checking in at the Holiday Inn, I began my morning prayer dedication at 5:40 a.m. I remember randomly placing my finger in my Bible and it landed directly on (Joel 1:14). That verse says: "Declare a holy fast; call a sacred assembly. Summon the elders and all who live in the land to the house of the Lord your God, and cry out to the Lord." Wow! This was confirmation for me! God had me "On Assignment!" Little did I know what would happen next? I emailed Pastor Derrick Faison (an old friend and Delaware native), Sean Smith and Curtis Hairston (all Potter's House Staff Members) in order to let them know that I was back in town. I awaited their response.

A mighty and powerful woman of God showed up and prayed for us, we called her Evangelist Paula. Before starting the event she prayed for us and told us the Conference would be bigger than we could ever imagine. God was about to open many doors for our National Recruitment Team. Evangelist Paula said we were special and instructed us to stay focused. She told us to be humble because this opportunity wasn't about us, but had everything to do with the building up of God's Kingdom. She also prayed for

Perfect Will Ministries in my absence and declared everything would be fine. She told me that she saw exponential growth for our Church in the future. Led by the Holy Spirit, she began to pray for my baby boy (Zachariah). She said he was special and would go on to do extra-ordinary things. This absolutely blew my mind.

Things started to change! People were now freely coming to our booth and requesting detailed information concerning employment with the FBI. I would now see what Evangelist Paula was talking about when she prophesied to us. At approximately 11:45 am, on Friday, March 30th, Sean Smith came to our table and approached James Atkinson and I. He said that they had noticed positive response received by the attendees. Sean told us that Bishop Jakes wanted us to address the General Assembly after lunch. Excuse me? I'm sorry, Mr. Smith, you said what? You mean stand up in front of 7,000 men and tell them what? Sean told me to tell what it was like to be a Special Agent with the FBI and a Pastor. He looked at me and said, "Apostle, I remember you from the S.TO.P.P.E.D training. Now I know why you executed the way you did. You didn't tell me you were a FBI Agent. Please Apostle, tell them what it's like to be an Apostle and an Agent." Therein lies the inspiration for this Book... thanks Sean!

So we did it, James went first and then I addressed the assembly. James spoke about what it was like to be an Afro-American Special Agent. I detailed what is was like to be in law enforcement and the ministry. We got a phenomenal response from the conference attendees. I would not trade that opportunity for the World. This was special. This was cutting edge.

We finished the Conference with outstanding reviews on that Saturday. Some of us decided to stay an extra day to attend Sunday Service at the Potter's House. On that Sunday we were escorted to special seating and in between the two morning services Bishop Jakes requested to see us. We went to his office and he thanked us for our efforts. He was very honest and told us that he was unsure what effect the FBI would have at his conferences. He said he was skeptical at first, but was glad it worked out. I had a chance to ask him some question regarding being a Pastor and he graciously answered each question I asked. We did not want to take too much of his time because the 2nd Service would be starting soon. At the end of our "chance" meeting he offered us a "carrot." He asked if our Team would be a part of other Conferences he would have in 2007. We humbly accepted. OMG! You mean, I would have an opportunity to work with Bishop Jakes again at different venues? This Year? 2007? Lord, please pinch me!

From May 21st to May 24th of 2007, our NRT had the opportunity to travel to Los Angeles, CA to support Bishop Jakes. He allowed us to be a sponsor at Bishop Charles E. Blake's elevation service, as presiding Bishop of the Church of God in Christ (C.O.G.I.C). Bishop Blake is the Pastor of the West Angeles Cathedral, which is one of the largest churches in the Western United States. He has a membership of 24,000. Bishop Blake has been recognized annually as one of the 100 + most influential Afro-Americans. Again, our recruitment effort was a success and after the Service the Team attended the V.I.P. after party. We met Bishop Blake and other celebrity guest members who attend his Church (Courtney Vance, Desiree Coleman, Bill Duke, Jonathan Slocumb, and Tom Lister, Jr – aka Tiny or Deebo from the movie Friday's).

You would never guess who showed up while we were in Los Angeles? Uh huh, you may have guess it correctly... Evangelist Paula. Sure enough, Evangelist Paula prayed for us before the event and even took us to the famous, ROSCOE'S CHICKEN & WAFFLES Restaurant (5006 W. Pico Blvd & S. Mansfield Ave, Los Angeles CA).

For some reason the Holy Spirit was urging me to go to Compton, CA. I asked for directions and made my way over to Compton. There again, was Evangelist Paula who had some affiliation with "Faith Inspirational" School asked if I would come and present to the students. She asked if I could simply speak some words of inspiration and encouragement to them. This school was made up of Middle and High School students from some of the roughest parts of Compton. There were Blacks, Latinos and a few White students. They were good young men and women who grew up in challenging environments. I spoke of many things to an auditorium full of bright, intelligent, attentive and hopefully students. As I closed, I challenged them to be great! Lord, now you have me clear across the Country ministering to young folk. I thought I came out for one thing, but you had something greater for me to do. Yes Lord, I hear You Loud and Clear... "Be instant in season and out of season."

Before departing, I had the opportunity to visit Watts (section), in the general area where Sanford and Son was taped. I got to see the amazing Watts Tower (a tower masterfully constructed of scrap metal) in the middle of a few city blocks. Amazing!

My final opportunity to serve Bishop T.D. Jakes in 2007 was from October 18th to the 20th. Our NRT was requested to be sponsors at Bishop's FOR WOMEN ONLY CONFERENCE. My wife, Pastor Tasey flew down to join me for this Conference. I had the opportunity to meet: Pastor Judy Jacobs, Trin-i-Tee 5:7, Martha Munizzi (this is where I would first cross paths with Martha), and Essence Magazine Editor in Chief – Susan L. Taylor. On Saturday, Bishop Jakes held an additional Conference call B.E.S.T. This was for Business Entrepreneurs and Black Men & Women Professionals. I attended Sunday Service at the Potter's House. Fred Hammond had just joined the Church and Dorothy Norwood was guest vocalist that day. What a Year! 2007 was full of Blessings!

Simultaneously, on March 29th while in Dallas, TX, I received a Certificate of Achievement Award for Special Efforts and Contributions to the FBI's Civil Rights Program. The certificate was signed by Director Mueller and was considered an "On-the-Spot" award. I began to receive invitations to speak on behalf of the Bureau as a Civil Rights expert. I would be the Civil Rights Coordinator for the Philadelphia Division for eight years and conduct presentations for various organizations.

I have already mentioned that I met Martha Munizzi and her husband Dan at the Bishop T.D. Jakes' – FOR WOMEN ONLY CONFERENCE in October of 2007. However, on Saturday, August 8, 2009 I had the unique opportunity to reconnect with them. I was doing Executive Security Detail for Pastor Gary Whetstone (Victory Christian Fellowship, New Castle DE), in lieu of his 25th ministerial anniversary. Since Bishop Jakes was coming to our vicinity (Mid-Atlantic area) and I had already established a rapport and credibility with his security detail, I along with another of my Staff was asked to assist this auspicious event. Minister Frank Elcock (Perfect Will Ministries, New Castle DE) and I supplemented Bishop Jake's Security Team because Bishop was the featured speaker on Thursday, August 6, 2009.

After providing service for Bishop Jakes on that evening, we ended up fellowshipping with Pastor Gary and Bishop Jakes after the event which was held at the 1st USA Center (now the Chase Center – Waterfront in Wilmington, DE). Pastor Gary's staff asked Minister Frank and I, if we did not mind taking the lead and helping them out for one more night because Pastor Donnie McClurkin was coming in. We agreed. On Friday, August 7th, Pastor McClurkin came to the Chase Center, along with Sean Slaughter (Alvin's Slaughter's son) and blessed the attendees. We got Pastor McClurkin back safely to his hotel, where I introduced Pastor Tasey to him. Again, Pastor Whetstone's staff asked if we could assist on the next night, because Martha Munizzi was scheduled. You know that I couldn't reject this offer. To have the opportunity to reunite with Martha would be fabulous.

On Saturday, August 8th, Martha arrived at the Chase Center. We greeted her and I re-introduced myself to her and Dan. She ministered well that evening and had everybody on their feet. Then the anointing of God simply descended up that Center and souls were saved and bondages broken. Just as the others had done before her, after they ministered they stuck around a bit to sign autographs and take photographs with the people. When the evening was over, we successfully returned Dan and Martha to their hotel.

Finally, staff asked us one more time and there were totally understanding that the next day was a Sunday. They asked if we could assist one more time because Pastor Rod Parsley was coming in. Understanding that I was a Senior Pastor and had to preach that day, if I rejected the offer they would totally understand. I agreed to serve once again. We enjoyed serving God's people.

On that Sunday morning, August 9th, I preached a Sermon entitled: "How's Your Heart?" I came from (2 Chronicles 26:1-4; 16-22). That evening, Minister Frank and I reported for duty to protect and serve. Pastor Rod came in and closed the Anniversary out with a bang! In his bold style, he began to minister to the hearts of the people and just like the nights before, people were saved. What an awesome weekend! We had the opportunity to serve some ministry greats and secure their safety.

The reason for listing the above, is to demonstrate that when dealing with "Infectious Encounters," something about the God in you immediately connects with the God in them. As a result of that ordained encounter... "Fruit" is developed.

2

THE TRAIN RIDE HOME

————⟨∞⟩————

"Every time you think you're being rejected for something good,
God is actually re-directing you to do something better."

The Bible states in (Ecclesiastes 7:8) that: "The end of a thing is better than its beginning." How true this would be for me in 2013.

After a 22 ½ stellar career as a veteran FBI Special Agent, little did I know that my train ride home on March 7, 2013 would be the beginning of an "end." Frustrated because of budget constraints and after all I had done in this hallowed organization, I was now relegated to taking the train back and forth to work. I was used to driving the 100 mile round trip from Delaware to Philadelphia every day, for 22 years. That was 500 miles per week and actually a lot more, depending on my assignments. I was used to having access to my car—I was a Hostage Negotiator, Media Representative, Employee Assistance Coordinator (EAP), and a Member of the Bureau's National Recruitment Team I needed access!

To have to take the train to work and back home? Me... an accomplished Agent, really? I never knew that God was orchestrating something huge and wonderful in my life. As a matter of fact, it was all for purpose and "on purpose" by God. While one door was closing, God was opening a whole different door that would entail fresh and new opportunities. In my irritation, I was blinded to all the blessings that God had bestowed on me. But on my train ride home on that day, God would garner my attention and begin to teach me a powerful lesson.

I began the day by catching the SEPTA Regional Rail Line Train (Wilmington/Newark Line – Train #2718) from Churchman's Crossing, DE to Center City Philadelphia (Market East Station). My train arrived in Delaware at 6:29 am and would get me to my destination at 7:42 am. I would walk several blocks and be at work by 7:55 am. During my train ride this morning, I was not able to see much because the sun did not come up until I was almost at work. As I started my day, embarrassed I did not have a car, I kept a really low profile. After all, I had just been the primary Media Representative for the Division. I was still the Coordinator for the EAP and a Hostage Negotiator. Again, seriously…no car? Can somebody say, "Humility?" I did not know that God would humble me through all of this.

As my work day ended, I had to get adjusted to my new work schedule (I would catch the 4:04 pm train from Market East Station). If this train was on time it would get me back to my stop in Delaware at 5:16 pm. If I missed that train, then the next train available for my stop would not come until an hour later and get me back in Delaware by 6:13 pm. There was no flexibility at all! Because I did not want to be bothered by anyone on the train, I quickly discovered that Monday through Friday between 4:00 am and 7:00 pm, the first car of the train was designated as a Quiet Ride Car. That meant any conversations had to be in a low-tone voice. No cell phone calls were allowed. No loud music or blaring headphones, and there were no screaming children allowed in this car. Yes!!! I wanted this time (one hour) to be a time where I could read God's Word and listen to whatever it was that He would have me to hear.

On this specific day, on this specific train ride home God asked me a question. He said, "So you are mad, huh?" I said "yeah!" He said, "Okay, then let me teach you a valuable lesson and show you the reason you are on this train. So just sit back, be quiet and observe." I caught the 4:04 at Market East, got on and sat in my designated Quiet Ride spot. As we went through Suburban Station (underground), we approached 30th Street Station. At this location, God brought back to my remembrance the many drug cases that I'd worked inside that very building conducting surveillance on bad guys who would come and go through this Station. As we approached the next station (University City), God showed me just a few years back I had one of the most high profile Hate Crime cases at Children's Hospital Of Pennsylvania (CHOP). I was the Civil Rights Coordinator at the time and it was a case where a white male, hung a noose and presented it to a black male. We pulled out of the University City stop and rolled through Darby, Curtis Park, Sharon Hill, Folcroft, Glenolden, Norwood, and Prospect Park stops.

In between the Ridley Park and Eddystone stops, God had me look over to my left side. I looked, and to my amazement it took me back to when I was a little boy. As a kid, I remember driving up that old highway (Rt. 291) and seeing where my Dad once worked. My Dad was a "blue-collar" worker who worked at Boeing. At Boeing, my Dad worked on the Boeing CH-47 Chinook Helicopter. They were the dual propeller helicopters that looked really cool flying in the air. And look! There was the machine that tested the propeller blades. It looked sort of different now. When I was a little boy it didn't have that cage surrounding the top.

Reflecting back in time, one day as my Mom, Sister and I were going to pick my Dad up from work, when we heard a loud bang. Suddenly our front windshield was smashed all over. As my Mom "Put the Pedal to the Medal" we honestly thought we were being shot at! We hurried and finally got to my Dad's job and later realized that a stone from the propeller tester had been lifted from the ground and propelled directly into our windshield. I'm still cracking up over that incident as I write about it today!

As I continued to look back on my youth and Boeing, God quickly brought back to my remembrance that this is the place where my Father labored very hard for my family. This is the place where Dad worked 1st, 2nd, and 3rd shifts just so we could be provided for. God reminded me that my Dad worked tremendously hard on our behalf and he never once complained.

Next stop, was Chester, PA. As I gazed out the window to my left I saw the Kimberly Clark Factory. Years ago, this same building was home to the Scott Paper plant. This is the place where my Mother labored for over 30 years. While my Dad worked at different Mills and Plants (due to layoffs), my Mom worked at "Scott's" consistently for more than 30 years. She too, worked all three shifts just like my Dad. I remember as a little boy being placed in the car and being driven up to the front gate waiting for my Mom to get off. Sometimes my sister and I would be asleep, but would always awaken to Mom's beautiful smiling face. We talked for a bit, take the drive back down to Delaware, then get back home and go to sleep for the evening. As I continued to stare at the building, God brought back to my remembrance of when I was a teen driver, how I would now drive to pick my Mom up from work. What a pleasure it was to have this responsibility to pick up the Queen that I loved. To "think it not robbery" of this time to dedicate it to the one who had sacrificed so much for me. When the train began to pull out of this stop I could feel myself begin to smile. What fond memories these were.

The next stop was Highland Avenue in Chester, PA. Between the Chester stop and Highland Avenue, it seemed as if my life were flashing before my eyes with fond memories. As I looked to the left side, there was my home church... the place that I had been rooted and grounded. The location was 4th and Edwards St. and the church was St. Daniels United Methodist Church. I began to reflect of how when I was a little boy, I stayed in trouble during the Services. I stayed in trouble because my cousins and I never paid attention to the Sermons, but always mocked the older folk in the church. For example, you had: "Leo the Lion." That was the older gentleman with the white hair and white sideburns that led Senior the mass choir. Every time the choir sang, his voice would drown out everyone else's and all you could hear was —- "Laaaaaaa – Laaaaaaa – Laaaaaaaaa!" He actually looked just like and sounded like the lion in the Wizard of Oz. So we began to imitate him and started cracking up, often times into a disturbing laughter! So, I along with my cousin Bob, got smacked in church a lot. Then you had the "Amen" Lady. This was an older lady who sat across from our isle (yes, we had our own row… the Simpson family pew was on the left hand side and the 4th row. If somebody else sat in that row that wasn't in our family… oh, you were in trouble!) So this older lady, every single week, would fall asleep during the Sermon. Her head would begin to nod, forward then backward… then side to side. But at certain points of the Sermon she would suddenly open her eyes and say, "Amen!" God brought back to my remembrance as I looked at St. Daniels, these were the best of times… and the worst of times. Yet, this was truly my starting point in Him. This was my foundation. As we continued to move forward I was able to locate the areas I used to live in: 8th and Lincoln St., 200 block of Yarnall St., 216 Yarnall St (my Grandmother's House); and the last place we lived in before moving to Delaware, was a small apartment on Minor St. at the intersection of Jeffrey St. Living in that apartment was Mom, Dad, my paternal Grandfather, my sister, and I. We moved out in 1969 after my Pop-pop Fernie passed away. As we continued along the line I looked over to my right and there was Memorial Park. It now had a community swimming pool that was not there when I was growing up, but the old baseball fields still remained. I remembered when I was only 4 years old and my Dad and Grandfather had me out on the field shagging down fly balls. I remember the shock on my Dad's face as I got under one of those huge softballs in Centerfield, put my glove would be and got him "smack-dab" in the middle of my face. Both my Father and Grandfather rushed out to see if I was okay. They I was, down and crying after taking a direct hit to the face. My Dad thought I would never play baseball again. But little did he know that God had a plan for my life and I would go on to finish tops in the Nation playing this beloved sport while in College. Passing Memorial park, also on my right side and up on a hill, was the place I was born. Whew, I had to take a deep breath! Sacred Heart Hospital in the vicinity of 9th and Highland Avenue, wow! The place was a lot different. Now known as Community Hospital, 2600 West 9th Street, you could see the old red brick building in the rear (Sacred Heart). I remember the countless times passing the place where I was born on my way to visit family members in Chester. This location was truly a landmark for me and represented a significant and true beginning in my life.

My attention was redirected back to the tracks as the train began to pull out of this stop. The next stop was the Marcus Hook station. Markus Hook was the place I remember my maternal Grandfather working. Pop-Pop Bus worked at the Sun Oil refinery. Each time I-95 was backed-up or there was a significant accident on the road, I would take this alternate route to get to and through Chester. As we made our way forward on the train, the next stop was Claymont. Claymont is a city in Delaware that is on the border line between PA and DE. I looked to my right and saw the location where the last known Drive-In Movie Theater in DE once stood on Naamans Rd. I remember going to the Naamans Drive-In with my Parents and Sister as a little boy. This Drive-In opened in 1968 and had a capacity to hold 800 cars. What I remember most about that Drive-In, was paying our admission fee, then driving very slowly through a gravel typed surface (you could actually hear the crackling as the tires met the gravel). I remember, then pulling up to an approximate 4 ft. pole with a big speaker on it. Once parked, you would take the speaker of the pole and then place the hook on the back of the speaker to your window if it was cold outside (you would roll the window all the way up and the speaker would hang on the inside of the vehicle). If it was hot outside, and we had a convertible, you would drop the top and hang the speaker on the door. During inter-mission, we would run back to the concession stand which was in the middle of the Drive-In, and purchase popcorn, candy, and soda. We would watch the latest movie on the huge 40ft by 50ft. screen. Most of the time our family would simply stop at Claymont Sub Shop and order jumbo cheesesteaks and hoagies before going to the Theater. This Drive-In closed in 1987 with a triple-feature showing. Wow, what awesome memories! I had chills as I passed this location.

As the train crossed the State line from PA into DE, we veered slightly to the left and began to pass the back side of Citi Steel. I'd never seen the back side of the building and what I saw was not good. It had holes all throughout the back side, which told me that conditions on the inside were probably deplorable at times. In the winter it prob-ably was brutal. And in the summer is was most likely so hot in there that you could fry and egg. This is the place that my Dad worked for a number of years after getting laid off from Boeing. I remember sitting in the car with my Mom and my Sister as we picked Dad up from the front side of what was then called Phoenix Steel. I had always known that the conditions on the inside were extreme because you could always see hot steel blazing when the doors were open. Never once, as a child did I ever consider the sacri-fice that my Dad made for us to live comfortably. Never once did I imagine the toll that the continuous loud noises would take on his hearing. Never once did I ever stop to think about the exposure of Coal Dust and what effect they could have on my Dad and his Co-Workers lungs. Oh my gosh!!! Dad did this all for us, what an incredible sacrifice! Now, here is the big deal with all of why I'm writing in such a detailed fashion about the places my Dad worked. My Dad was a hard worker and worked sometimes around the clock. However, Dad rarely missed anything big that I participated in. He was always at my games (Football, Basketball, and Baseball). Even in College where I played Football and Baseball... Dad was always there! He made all my Graduations. He was there at my ministry licensing and ordinations. This definitely set a precedent for how I would shadow my life concerning my children.

With just a few stops to go after departing the Claymont Station, I looked over to my right and there was the place where I first met my wife (Tasey). I remember the address well, 1349 Prospect Drive (Cambridge Apartments) near Edgemore, DE. As I looked up that little hill I remembered going to my wife's apartment for the very first time. She could not stand my guts! She said I was too loud and cocky. My, oh my, look what the Lord has done 25 years later. There is a God! Can I get a witness?

As we continued I saw my old "stomping grounds" growing up. There was the Edgemore Movie Theater which was an indoor movie theater with only two screens and theaters. Across the street was the "Merchandise Mart" Shopping Center where we used to ride our bikes to and hang out. Behind the Shopping Center and up on the hill was the First State Lanes Bowling Center. This was the place I learned how to bowl. Moving along and to the right side still, I could see the area where my wife grew up (the Purina Chow building was a long standing landmark there). Good old 35th Street! Many of my friends grew up on this block. As I looked a little further out into the distance, I could see my old High, Middle, and Elementary Schools. They were all in the general vicinity where I grew up in. Passing all of them left many warm memories deep down on the inside.

As we approached the Wilmington Train Station, I looked to my right and directly on the other side of the tracks was the Riverside Projects. I'd forgotten all about this memory. I'd forgotten that this was another beginning for me. There it was, Kingswood Community Center (in the Riverside Section) and the field behind it was the place I started my football career. I was 12 years old and would walk from West 39th Street over to E. 23rd and Bowers Street just to participate on the Trojans football team. The first day of practice was so hard that me and my buddy (Petey) decided to quit. We decided that all that running and acting like we were in Military Boot Camp was not for us, we simply would not go back. However, when I told my Dad about my wishes... he looked me straight in the eye and said: "I ain't raising no quitters! Now you go back and finish what you've started!" Turned out, football would also be very crucial in attaining my College Degree. Finally, we pulled into the Wilmington Train Station. This is the same station I remembered seeing, Vice-President of the United States – Joseph R. Biden. He would catch the train to Washington D.C. Vice President Biden would ride the train to work every day when he was a United States Senator. I had known V.P. Biden since I was in High School while playing sports.

As the train made a stop at this station, I looked over to my right side and there was he Wilmington Courthouse. Just a few days prior there was a huge shooting inside the entrance of the Courthouse, which gained National Media attention (Monday, February 11, 2013). Two men died in that shooting that day, and God began to show me (even though I did not know it at the time) that He was preparing an exit strategy for me from law enforcement. Right before we were about to pull out enroute to my final destination, I looked over to my left and saw a Street sign at the corner of the train station that read: "ROSA PARKS DR." It is a short road between the train station and the Tubman-Garrett Riverfront Park. This landmark Park was named after Thomas Garrett who lived in a nearby Wilmington neighborhood (Quaker Hill), where slaves often traveled the Underground Railroad and found refuge and for the fellow abolitionists Harriett Tubman. God snapped me back and quickly reminded me that in no way should I be complaining for having to ride the train back and forth to work. It let me know that I was a spoiled brat. It caused me to take my attention off myself and all my accomplishments and think about the greats that had gone before me, who made it possible for me to even get on the train. After, thinking about Garrett, Tubman and Parks... I began to feel really small. I felt inadequate. So as we made our approach to my final stop (Churchman's Crossing), I felt a sense of gratitude. I was grateful for all the things that God had shown me! I was thankful that the Lord had reminded me "from whence I had come." As I got into my car and headed home, I had a new-found appreciation and did not feel worthy to complain anymore.

When I pulled up into the driveway of my nice house and pushed the button to open my garage, the voice of God spoke again and said: "How dare you complain about having to ride the train after 22-years in the FBI! I gave you that Career that I might be glorified. Look at where you rest your head at night, look at what I have allowed you to provide for your wife and children. You have raised your children in a well-to-do and multicultural neighborhood. People died so that this would come to pass and you, as a Civil Rights Coordinator with the FBI, fought for it. DON'T YOU DARE SECOND GUESS ME AGAIN... EVER!" Needless to say, I never complained or thought about complaining again. However, I would embrace the time that the Lord would have me in transit via the train. All the time God was preparing me for greater, but I would have to walk in obedience.

3

MY PLAN

———*oOo*———

"If you want to make God laugh, tell Him your plans." – Woody Allen

In 1969 my family uprooted from Chester, PA and moved to Wilmington, DE. It was Mom and Dad, my sister and me. I was six years old and I started playing baseball in the Wilmington Optimist Little League which was located off of 18th and Broom St. Back then I played Shortstop and Pitcher and every year I played, I made the All-Star Team. From the ages of six to twelve I had the honor to represent the League as an All-Star and got the chance to compete against other All-Stars from around the Region. When I was thirteen years old, I continued to play baseball for a 13-15 Year old Babe Ruth League Team. I still played Shortstop and pitched a little bit, but I was blessed to be an All-Star in this League for three years as well. By the time I turned 16 years old, I continued to play Summer League baseball in a 16-18 League. I was also participating in High School baseball. In High School the Coaches moved my position to Center Field because of my speed and ability to easily track the ball. In the 16-18 League, I played for a team named Brooks Armored Cars. Our Coach was Ed Pankowski (an older gentleman). Ed was a fiery old man and had a long reputation of winning. Coach Ed changed my position to Center Field as well and I started at that position for the three years I played for him. During my three year tenure, Brooks Armored Car won the Championship each year. And from the time Coach Ed had the team (approximately 14 years), Brooks never finished lower than second place in the League.

Prior to High School, the only other organized sport I played was Football. At 12 years old, I was a member of the Wilmington Trojans Football Team, which I had mentioned earlier. Coach Levy, Coach Moon, Coach Hawk, and the other Coaches really pushed us to be great at such a young age. I was a bigger kid for my age, but was very agile so I started at fullback. We went undefeated that year and many of my Trojan teammates would go on to excel in High School Football, some College and others made it to the Pros. The Wilmington Trojans had a tremendous run and went undefeated for about 10 years! Anybody who wanted to be somebody, if they were from our area, wanted to play for the Trojans.

While in High School, I competed on the Varsity Baseball, Football and Basketball teams. In my freshman year I attended P.s. DuPont High School in Wilmington. At the beginning of my sophomore year the State of Delaware incorporated mandatory Busing policy (deseg-regation), so I was assigned to go to Brandywine High School in North Wilmington. This was a very difficult year and a year of transition for many of the students, teachers and parents. It was a year that entailed lots of tension because we did not want to be bussed out to the "white" schools and many of the people did not want us out there. I remember the very first day we arrived at Brandywine High, there where white parents standing out in front of the school protesting our arrival. They were screaming and shouting all sorts of things (I won't even bother to repeat) and they had picket signs signifying their displea-sure of us being there. It was very intense! I remember thinking, "God please help us to endure!" As I reflect back on it now... Wow! We were only kids, we didn't ask to be there. However, because I was a good athlete and did well on my High School teams, it gave me immediate credibility with the city kids and the suburban kids. Even back then I was sort of a mediator and a type of negotiator for several parties. I was also observing potential Civil Rights issues. Little did I know that God was using these experiences to prepare me for later in life?

In High School Baseball I was a starter and Captain. I played Centerfield and made the Delaware All-Conference Teams for a couple of years. On the High School Football Team, I was also team Captain. I played Quarterback, Wide Receiver and Safety. In my Junior and Senior Years I made the All-Conference and All-State Teams and when I was a senior, I was selected to play in the Blue-Gold Football Game. The Blue-Gold Game was a High School All-Star game where the best players from the Northern part of Delaware compete against the best in the South. I played for the Blue Team (North) along with three of my High School Teammates. I was not a very good Basketball player at all. In reality, I thought Basketball was kind of a ridiculous game where you ran up and down the court trying to put a little ball through a hoop. I did play street ball growing up as a kid. In our neighbor-hood we would play at Harlan Elementary, Haines Park, or P.s. DuPont Courts. If you were of better caliber then you would venture out and play at Prices Corner Basketball Courts. However, I never played organized basketball until I got into the 9th grade. I just wanted something to keep me in shape between Football and Baseball season. By the time I arrived at Brandywine High School in the 10th Grade, I started to like Basketball a bit more and made the varsity team in my sophomore, junior, and senior years. But Baseball and Football were still my favorites.

By the time I was a senior in High School, my High School Football Coach – Mr. Steve Lennox, was sending letters off to Colleges who might want to recruit me.

One of his letters read:

"I have an outstanding prospect who is interested in attending your University. He has just completed his junior year and may be able to visit this summer if you are interested. He has his senior year of High School left and one more year of eligibility.

His name is Frank Burton, Jr. He is an outstanding wide receiver and free safety. Frank possesses outstanding speed and hands which helped him earn All-Conference and All-State Honors. Presently he is 6'0" and 180 lbs. He is also the Centerfielder on the Varsity Baseball Team. He possesses a great attitude and has a tremendous desire to succeed. He would definitely be an asset to your program."

When my senior year arrived at Brandywine High, our Quarterback had graduated so the Coach asked me if I would play Quarterback. Being a "team player" and willing to do whatever it took in order for our team to win, I agreed. On October 1, 1980 the headline article in the Delaware Evening Journal read: "Brandywine discovers QB answer in Burton." Remember, I had just made All-Conference and All-State at Wide-Receiver and my goal in my senior year was to continue to be successful and make a higher All-State team, at that position. Tom Cobourn, the Sports writer of that article stated:

"Frank's individual goal was to make All-State as wide receiver, said Coach Renzi... and why not? Burton caught close to 40 passes a year ago with fluid, stylish moves, great speed and fingers of fly paper. If there were any receivers better than Burton returning for the 1980 season they would do just as well going hardship and running a quick post right into the National Football League. However, Burton added and important footnote on his card. His second goal was to play Quarterback... if needed."

Long-story-Short, I received a Full Four-Year Athletic Scholarship to Delaware State College (back then and is now a University) to play football. I was also allowed to play on my College's Baseball Team and was the Captain for all the years I played. In 1984, as of May 30th, I was a NCAA Division I Leader in Stolen Bases. Published in Street and Smith's Baseball Magazine, I was 9th in the Nation in the Stolen Bases Leader category. I graduated in four years, playing two sports, with a GPA of 3.25. My Plan was to go straight to the Pros after leaving College.

However, I'm certain that God was smiling just watching all of "My Plans" unfold because He had a totally different direction for me. The first of which, would be a humbling process.

4

IN THE BEGINNING

—⟨∿⟩—

*"If God shuts a door STOP banging on it! Trust whatever
is behind it... is not meant for You!"*

Needless to say, I did not make it to the Pros. Life threw me a few curveballs and I
did not quite navigate some things very well, so I graduated from College in May of
1985 came home and secured a job. My very first job (I'd never worked before because
all my life was dedicated to playing sports) was at a bank named – The 1st National Bank
of Wilmington. This bank was located in Ogletown, DE. I went through the training and
started out as a Collector, but that only lasted one day after my very first caller cussed
me out over the phone. My natural instinct was to react to this caller, in kind. But, I
knew that all calls were being recorded, so I just told the gentleman that if he really
had an issue and wanted to do terrible things to me, then he knew where to find me
and we could get things done! My Supervisor overheard the call and beckoned me to
her Office. She said Frank, "you seem to be a good worker, level headed even... but you
can't react to the callers in that fashion." So she moved me to the Security Department
where we dealt with fraudulent Credit Cards and the Nigerian Fraud Ring. My boss was
a gentleman named William (Bill) Rhodunda. Bill was a retired Secret Service Agent and
had taken this job as a retirement position. I also worked with two other retired Police
Officers (William "Bill" Osowski – Wilmington Police Department and Mike Rogers – New
Castle County Police Department) in the Security Department.

One day, Bill sat me down and said to me: "Frank you are very smart and artic-
ulate. You pay close attention to detail and write very well. Have you ever thought
about becoming a Secret Service Agent?" I looked at Bill all wide eyed and replied: "Bill,

you know a City Boy, right? All I know about the Secret Service is that you all protect Presidents and when people pull out guns to try to assassinate them, you guys jump in front of their bullets!" I said, "No thanks Bill! That's not in my order of short term or long term plans. Appreciate it, Sir!" Bill explained that the Secret Service did more than protective details but also dealt with treasury issues and investigations. I still told him, "Thanks... but, No Thanks!" As time went by, I began working with the FBI, Secret Service, and the local Law Enforcement Agencies on the different cases we had at the Bank. I started to get familiar with the nomenclature and liked the interaction with Law Enforcement. I liked what I was doing at the Bank although the pay was not very much, especially for what I thought a College Graduate should receive... for the most part I enjoyed the work.

Bill came to me one day and advised that the FBI was testing in Wilmington, DE and I should go down and take the test. I agreed and went. When I arrived to take the test I was greeted by a nice young lady. She sat me and a large group of others into a classroom like setting. She talked about the three hour test that was before us. She explained how the test would be broken down into different parts and then she showed us this video. This video was scary! It almost made me want to leave the moment it ended. The video started out with approximately 100 people (male and females) standing out in the grass in front of a building at Quantico, VA. The men were nicely dressed in suits and the ladies had on business attire (dresses and skirt sets). A voice on the video began to speak and said: "If you've ever used drugs you will be disqualified... If you've ever been convicted of a crime you will be disqualified... If you have bad credit... if you cannot pass these fit requirement... and so on and so on —- if you can't do this you will be disqualified." The scariest thing about this movie was that after every disqualifier... a few people would just disappear. By the time the movie was complete, out of the 100 people, there were only 7 people left standing. These mere seven people were the ones who qualified to continue on with the strenuous process. If I'm being honest right now, this really freaked me out! I had to catch my breath to continue. I had to totally regroup and refocus on the written test that was at hand. Because I was not serious about taking this test (I only did it as a challenge to see if I could do well), I finished in about an hour and a half. When I got up and turned my test in, many of the people present looked at me like I had two-heads. As I walked away, the facilitator said "Thank You!" And told me if my scores were competitive I would be contacted to proceed to Phase Two, which was an oral interview. In the summer of 1991, I received my invitation to attend the FBI Training Academy at Quantico, VA. I was a member of the prestigious Class 91-17. In November of 1991 I was assigned to the Philadelphia Division. I spent my entire FBI Career assigned to that particular office.

5

GODS PRESENCE

—◦∕∕◦—

"Sometimes, burning a bridge is not such a bad thing. It will keep you from going back to a place you never should revisit again!"

1997 would be the year that literally changed my life! I was 34 years at the time and seeking a closer relationship with the Lord. Being over thirty years old I had now journeyed in to the spiritual realm of what the "mature male" was supposed to be. The number 30 represents "maturity" in the spirit. In my life I had some "ups" and some "downs," many victories and a few devastating defeats, but for the most part my life was going smoothly. 1997 started out with a "Bang!" On February 28th my wife took a pregnancy test and it resulted positive. It was confirmed on March 3rd after I took her to Med-Lab for a blood test. We were pregnant again and very excited!

I was a Team Leader on the Philadelphia Division's Special Operations Group (SOG) during this period and my team was assigned to work all over the place. At the beginning of 1997 we were working cases in the Philadelphia/South Jersey vicinity. In May of 1997 I led our SOG team up to the South Bronx, NY to work on a case. At the end of May, I was called to testify in court on a case I had worked previously. So my days were full and we were very busy. On July 10th there was some talk about us having to respond to a Special Operations Response Team (S.O.R.T.) trip to Denver, Colorado. Denver was the place selected to host the Oklahoma City Bombing Trial. It was speculated that our assignment would be to travel to Denver in order protect the families called to testify and make certain they were not bothered by the public. It was basically a Security Detail for the families.

There was one problem, though... my wife was currently six months pregnant with our second child and I did not want to be clear across the Country if she had any complications. I went to my supervisor and asked if I could be excused from this S.O.R.T. trip due to my family's present condition. My supervisor stated that he would ask our Special Agent in Charge (SAC) of the Philadelphia Division and get back with me. The word came down from the SAC that it was not possible because I was the Team Leader who had successfully commandeered our SOG squad on my previous missions. So my mind was heavy on that issue knowing that I could possibly be on the other side of the Country during my wife's pregnancy. After all, I was used to always being there for my family.

As time went on, I volunteered to assist with other Law Enforcement Officers (LEO's) for the Pastor Greg Laurie, HARVEST CRUSADE, which was held at the Spectrum Arena in South Philadelphia. The date was July 12th and it was a Saturday evening. We all got to meet Pastor Greg before the Crusade began. We ate, prayed together and then the event began. It was absolutely phenomenal to see a stadium filled to capacity (approximately 18,168 people) with believers of Jesus Christ! I had never experienced anything like this before and it actually served as a beginning, a launch, a starting point of my Executive Protection experience (of God would miraculously bless me with 10 years later). After Pastor Greg's teaching, thousands of people responded to the altar call and gave their lives to Christ. Incredible! I will never forget this "launching pad" experience. Little did I know that God was using these experiences to prepare me for the "Ministry."

In the Bible, Job said: "For the thing which I greatly feared is come upon me, and that which I was afraid of is come unto me." (Job 3:25) KJV. It happened! On Tuesday, August 12, 1997, I boarded a flight along with my SOG Team to Denver, CO. We departed Philadelphia on flight# 1227 at 12:35 am Eastern Time, and arrived in Denver at 1:24 pm Pacific Time. I was not happy a happy camper, having to separate from my wife at this time. When I got there I was even more upset after finding out what our assignment consisted of. To be honest with you, we were nothing more than glorified baby sitters. Let me give you a little bit of background to help you understand the awesomeness of God.

This was the very first time in my six -year FBI career that I was not undercover or using an assumed name. I was FRANK BURTON, JR. the FBI Agent and everybody in that vicinity knew it. They knew who we were and what we were there for. I was used to nice undercover vehicles that blended in with my surroundings, but we all were in big black Chevy Suburban's or Tahoe's. I literally felt like the "Men in Black" with all eyes on us. Our assignment was not to engage with the families, but sit out in front of the Magnolia Hotel and in the back alley to make sure that they were not disturbed by the general public. Also, we were directed to make certain that their "comings and goings" were undisturbed. Talking about being ticked? I was vexed, knowing that I had made this trip across the Country, leaving my six-months pregnant wife to sit in a vehicle that everybody knew who I was and what I was doing! "Uggghhhh!"

The Magnolia Hotel, 826 17th Street, was located on the corner of 17th and Stout Street, in Denver, CO. This Hotel is where all the family members participating in the OKC Trial were housed. It was a nice hotel in the middle of downtown Denver. Now, Denver is sort of like the New York City of the West. It was a place that had a lot of activity and many people visited this City. It had very nice places and some not so nice places. It was also the "Runaway/Homeless Capitol" of the West from what I experienced. There were very affluent people we came in contact with, but there was also a huge number of homeless people present. The way the Hotel sat, the front side of it (on Stout Street) was very clean and safe. The back side of the Hotel (17th St. alley) was a different story. Many homeless people frequented this alley. Drug transactions were conducted in this there and alcoholics generally could be observe here. Our SOG Team's assignment was approximately to cover a two week period. As I started to divide up the assignments for the Team Members, there was some conflict about who would cover the alley and who would be assigned to the front. To quell added tension and being the Team Leader... I advised that my partner and I (SA Bob Wineriter) would cover the alley and the rest could watch the front. Our shift was from 12:00 Midnight to 7:00 am.

SA Wineriter and I shared something very special in common. He was an older, experienced, white male Agent and I was a young, black male Agent. But we both loved the Lord! We both spoke very highly of our Lord and Savior, Jesus Christ and were not ashamed of it. How ironic, now that I think about it at this time, that his nickname was "Wino." People called him this because nobody wanted to annunciate his entire last name – Wineriter. "Wino" and I set up in the alley 12:00 midnight, did our detail while remaining vigilant. We spent many nights testifying to each other about the glory of God. Directly across the street from the Magnolia Hotel alley was two very active night clubs (The "Club" was representative of a "bridge." It was a bridge that God was burning in my life, showing me it was a place that I should never revisit again). For one solid week I had a front row seat to the utter nonsense that takes place at these nightclubs (the fights, disputes, drunkenness, cheating, disregard for women, drugs and chaos that surrounds this night spots). This was all a part of my past. I thought that the "Club" was the place to be, the place where all the fun goes down. God was showing me something as I studied these two spots every night for the first 7 days.

On the very first night of our assignment, shortly after our 12:00 midnight shift began, "Wino" and I were confronted by this homeless and alcoholic male that I'll call "Jimmy." "Wino" was in the driver's side and I was seated in the front passenger seat. It was mid-August, so it was hot outside. I had on shorts and cotton-shirt. I also wore a tan "fishing type" jacket covering to conceal my shoulder strapped holster I was wearing.

"Jimmy" approached the driver's side window and initiated a dialogue with "Wino." The conversation was much to do about nothing, just small talk. "Jimmy" did two things that I absolutely hated... he smoked cigarettes and he was drunk. I hated cigarettes (the smell of them makes me puke) and I don't care much for alcohol. Every evening, just like clock-work "Jimmy" would appear out of the alley at 12 midnight and began conversation with "Wino" and I.

On the eleventh day (Spiritually, eleven symbolizes: "End, Finish; Last Stop.") day of our S.O.R.T. trip, I had a day off and a group of guys decided to venture off and visit PIKE'S PEAK MOUNTAIN in Colorado Springs, CO. There were four of us, including "Wino." As we took the beautiful scenic drive down highway I-25 we marveled at the sights. The West Coast was so much different than the East Coast. They had real mountains, not those little 6,000 feet high hills we had back East. They also had things we learned about in elementary and middle school, but never really saw. The Plateaus (or Mesas as they call them), looked just like that... giant tables springing up out of seemingly nowhere. It was crazy to have read about them in our school books, but now to see them "up-close and personal" was altogether different. I remembered as a kid seeing commercials that had a Moose as their mascot. I never really paid much attention to those commercials, but it was quickly bought back to my attention when driving down I-25 early in the morning, I spotted a Moose. Because it was in between the night and dawn, I did not really recognize what I was seeing so I pulled the Tahoe over to the side of the road and backed up just to get a view of this amazing animal. This joker was huge! It was almost as big as the vehicle! I could not believe my eyes! This city boy was seeing things he had never seen before and it was blowing my mind.

We continued on down this 68-mile trip (took approximately 1 hour and 7 minutes), we stopped at the Air Force Academy and Garden of the Gods. We took several pictures at each location. Garden of the Gods was beautiful. It had several red-rock natural formations that were created during a geological upheaval along a natural fault line millions of years ago. This place was steep in History with evidence showing that pre-historic people visited the Garden of the Gods as far back as 1330 B.C. It is believed that approximately 250 B.C. Native Americans people camped in the park. However, the main attractions in the Garden were very unique structures called "The Three Graces" and "The Balanced Rock." "The Three Graces" were three step red-rock structures that almost looked like parts of a Praying hand. The "Balanced Rock" was one of the wonders of the World for me. It was a huge red-rock structure that appeared to be connected to a very small rock at its base, almost appearing to be balancing itself on its base. You could see where it physically connected on a small portion but could not believe that the weight and enormity of the top did not just cause the rock to topple over. God was already blowing my mind by saying: "Look at what I built! Embrace my beauty and the canvass I've selected to use." Wow!

(The ENCOUNTER that literally changed my life!)

We finally arrived at Pike's Peak Mountain. At the base we were at 5,000 feet above sea level (a Mile High). The top of the Mountain and elevation was 14,110 ft. This was the highest mountain I had ever seen in my life, personally. At its base there were pretty green evergreen trees and a large colorful billboard advertising: THE NORTH POLE – Home of Santa's Workshop. It had a big picture of Santa Clause in a red suit pointing the way and the sign stated that it was a gift shop which was "Fun for the Entire Family." I kept thinking to myself, "A Santa Claus Shop, what's up with this? It's the middle of August and the temperatures are in the mid to high 80's. What gives?" So we started the ascent up the Mountain. The drive took us in on a narrow serpentine road around the mountain and the total time it took to reach the summit was approximately two hours. As we got closer to the summit the scarcer and more bare the mountain became. We had the opportunity to see Yellow Belly Ferrets and Big Horn Sheep that lived on the mountain. The Big Horn Sheep were funny and amazing at the same time. Their grayish/white color blended in with the mountainous terrain, so when a vehicle would pass, they would just FREEZE and remain motionless until the vehicle passed. As they would freeze, you would really have to look hard to see where there were located on the mountain. It was almost like the game, "Where's Waldo?" A friend of mine and I got out and took pictures to demonstrate them blending in with the scenery. It was fantastic. When we finally approached 13,000 feet on the mountain the voice of God instructed me to pull over and get out. I was driving so I pulled over and got out. I had a friend of mine take a picture at that elevation where I was sitting on a rock with the mountains behind me. You could also see a beautiful blue lake in the background. I turned to go back to the vehicle and God spoke. He said: "This is what Jesus saw when he was tempted in Matthew Chapter 4. When the devil took him up on a mountain and told him that if Jesus would just bow down to him, he could own everything that he saw." How stupid was the devil? Trying to give Jesus something that he did not even own, yet and still, Christ already owned it all! God showed me how Jesus stayed the course and never gave into temptation and the devils lies. God explicitly told me that the entire desert experience was to test Jesus on three points: 1) His identity; 2) His Lifestyle; and 3) His Destiny.

His Identity – After Jesus was led by the Spirit into the desert to be tempted by the devil and after forty days and forty nights of fasting He was hungry. The Bible instructs us that the tempter came and tested Him by saying: "If you be the Son of God, tell these stones to become bread." Here was an outright and blatant test of Jesus' identity because in Matthew Chapter 3, after John the Baptist baptized Jesus the Bible says:

"He went up out of the water. At that moment heaven was opened, and he saw the Spirit of God descending like a dove and landing on him. And a voice from heaven said, 'THIS IS MY SON whom I love' and with Him I am well pleased." (vs. 16-17)

God already spoke before the heavens and all earth that Jesus was indeed His Son, but "old slew foot" decided to test Him on his identity. And that's just what the devil does with us today, especially men... he questions the fact that we are indeed sons of God and belong to Him.

After testing Jesus' identity, Jesus swiftly answered the devil by saying: "It is written: Man does not live by bread alone, but by every word that proceeds from the mouth of God." This is a direct quote from the scriptures in (Deuteronomy 8:3). It signifies that man is a spiritual being as well as a physical being, therefore we are to depend solely on God for our needs. In other words Jesus was saying, "Seriously, dude. I am hungry and haven't eaten in 40 days and 40 nights... but I don't need bread. You will not appeal to my flesh and I won't do anything just to prove to you who I am, because I know who I am... I am His!"

His Lifestyle – not being successful on his first attempt, the devil decides to test Jesus, once again. The Bible advises that the enemy then took Jesus to the Holy City and had him stand on the Highest Point of the Temple and he said: "If you be the Son of God, then throw yourself down because it is written that the He will command his angels concerning you and they will lift you up in their hands, so that you will not strike your foot against a stone."

That serpent is a crafty little sucker! Watch this:

This shows that the how much Satan knows the Bible, but he still thinks he can circumvent the Word of God. What he said was a direct reference to (Psalm 91:11-12). Angels did constantly help Christ as witnessed in (Matthew 4:11 and Luke 4:10-11). However, the devil corrupted the Scripture by leaving out the words: "in all your ways," and suggested it was "at any time." Come on people, the Bible says we have to "be as wise as serpents and as gentle as doves!" The devil is out to deceive us at all times that's why it is so very important that we know the truth. We need to be familiar with God's word and God's truth's because those who are familiar with the Truth... will more readily recognize a lie and error. The Messiah's path through the desert of the Wilderness was one of dependence on God. Satan's effort was to move Jesus to a place of reckless living.

In the same fashion, the devil challenges our lifestyle as Christians today! We know who we are and Who's we belong to, but he challenges us to live recklessly. A little bit of pornography is okay, just as long as nobody catches you! You don't have to physically cheat on your wife, men of God... not now. You don't even have to go out and buy sleazy magazines or books. Just click onto your computer and there before you in that 17" to 25" Screen is everything you desire. Cheat all you want and you don't have to go far to get it. Not physical... but emotional affairs are the devil's weapon of choice these days. You spend more time with your video vixen now, than you do with your wife. As a matter of fact, your wife doesn't turn-you-on anymore because you are trapped in the excitement that your newly created fantasy world presents. And forget about what God says in (Isaiah 29:13): "They honor me with their mouths but their hearts are far from me."

Somebody is saying right now, I don't believe it Apostle Frank. I don't believe that we as Christians fall for that "Lifestyle Trick!" Then please explain to me why the divorce rate in the Church has exceeded that of the World? Help me to understand that why it is, we have the numbers spike to astronomical rates of purchased pornography channels and X-rated movies during Christian Conferences and Convocations? Hotels report a spike in their Adult Channel viewership during this period. The devil is very cunning and will challenge our lifestyle on every front. On the other end of living recklessly, one man says, "Listen, I know I may have a problem with drinking or drugs… but I never do it in front of my children. I never let them see what I'm doing!" Okay, so does that make your reckless lifestyle okay? According to your skewed morals and values, it might. But the Word of God cannot lie! God's Word says: "I, the Lord your God, am a jealous God, punishing the children for the sin of the parents to the third and fourth generation of those who hate me, but showing love to a thousand generations to those who love and keep my commandments." (Exodus 20:5-6) This simply says that if you follow God's precepts and concepts then He will bless generations of yours (generational blessings); however, if you do not, then He will curse parents to the third and fourth generation of the parents (generational curses). But, Jesus answered: "It is also written: Do not put the Lord your God to the test." This is also in the Word and from (Deuteronomy 6:16). To tempt God is to question His word, which in effect, you are casting doubt on His ability to do what He has promised.

His Destiny – Jesus third and final temptation in the Wilderness was targeted at His Destiny. The Bible states that the devil again took Jesus to a very high mountain and showed him all the kingdoms of the World and their splendor. The devil said: "All this I will give you, if you will just bow down and worship me." This was the temptation that if successful, Christ would forfeit the Cross in which He would eventually rule and reign over all things after its completion. The devil does the same with us when he says: "If you forfeit your right to be parents… if you abort that child; If you become a cheat and unethical in your practices than you will gain everything that I want to give you; if you stop living for God and do what you want to … just keep listening to me, I will give you your heart's desire!" Well, that's an absolute lie from the "Pit of Hell." The Bible says: "What profit a man to gain the whole world, yet lose his soul?" (Mark 8:36). Is Hell really worthy losing eternity for? Eternity in Heaven is your destiny, you know that, right? The Bible also instructs that if we don't follow God, He will do a very bad thing and "turn us over to our reprobate mind." (James 1:28). The people did not think it was worthwhile to retain the knowledge of God, so God just turned them over to their own depraved minds and let them destroy themselves. Jesus' final answer to this third and final test from Satan was: "Get behind me Satan, for it is written: Worship the Lord your God, and serve him only." This is a direct reference from the Word of God in Deuteronomy as well. It comes from (Deuteronomy 6:13) and Jesus is directly address Satan now and letting him know that he had better "scram!" Then the Bible lets us know that the devil left Jesus for a season and the Angels came and ministered to Christ.

God allowed me in that pause on this particular mountain to see His splendor and majesty of how beautiful what He created and how Holy it was. It was a clear day and you could physically see the print of the city of Denver which was approximately 68 miles away. God was speaking, but He wasn't through. After that, God instructed me to turn around. I turned and saw a mountainous structure that appeared to be a stairway to the heavens. What I didn't realize is, I had taken a picture of this. It is not like today when you take a digital picture and you see the results right away. This was 35 millimeter camera that you had to take the film to the shop to get developed. When I received the picture back you could see the height of the rock formation tilting toward Heaven. At the very top of the frame is a large white and fluffy cloud surrounding the top of the mountain and when you look at the picture very closely you can see a rainbow typed figure between the rocks and the clouds. I was in awe. Unbelievable! The Lord then instructed me to get back into the vehicle and complete the climb to the summit, which was another one thousand feet high. We all re-entered the Tahoe and continued around the winding road until we reached the top of the mountain. What was crazy is that I began to sing in my mind a song that we used to sing back in elementary school and I could understand why? The words that came to me were: "Oh beautiful for spacious skies, for amber waves of grain. For purple mountains majesty above the fruited plain... America! America! God shed its grace on thee and crown thy good with brotherhood, from sea to shining sea." What? Where in the heck did that come from? I had not sung that song or even thought about it in over 25 years. What was up with that?

We finally arrived at the top of the mountain and the first thing we were greeting with was a large sign that sat on top of a rock formation and it read: SUMMIT PIKES PEAK, 14,110 FT. Pike National Forest. I remember that the elevation was so high that it was hard to really catch your breath (God literally took my breath away). At the bottom of the mountain they had warned that if you were pregnant or had heart problems you should probably not take the trip up the mountain. The first thing we saw was the Red Train that you could take to get to the top of the mountain. It stopped near a Rest Area/ Gift Shop building. We got out, stretched, and started to walk over to what appeared to be some sort of Monument. There it was! The reason I was singing that crazy old song. It was a Monument resurrected on behalf of Katherine Lee Bates. Bates was an English teacher from Massachusetts who decided to take a summer teach assignment at a College in Colorado Springs, CO in 1893. Bates was 34 years old and during her 2,000 mile train ride from Chicago to Colorado Springs, she became impressed by what she saw. After she visited Pike Peak (she took a carriage ride to the top) she wrote a poem titled: "America the Beautiful." The same things I saw, Mrs. Bates witnessed. The "Amber Waves of Grain" was the view you saw at the top of the mountains. From peak to peak the color of the tops of the mountains appeared to be amber and because of the numerous mountain chains connected (Rocky Mountains are the largest chain of mountains in the World. Colorado has 53 peaks over 14,000 ft. and about 250 peaks over 13,000 ft. Their horizon equals about 38 miles), they appeared to be in the formation of waves. "The Purple Mountains," didn't mean that there were any purple mountains, but the shadows contrasted off of the amber color and made the mountains in the distance appear to be purple. It was absolute a beautiful sight. Also at the top of the mountain was a Monument to Commemorate Olympic Athletes and there were plaques with names of famous Olympic athletes on them (Boxing: Leon and Michael Spinks, Howard Davis, and Ray Leonard). Each Olympic sport was represented with the perspective American Athletes names. Just for reference, in April of 1997 the United States Olympic Complex in Colorado Springs officially dedicated and opened its $23.8 million Phase II facilities, the home base where all our Olympic athletes train.

The guys and I looked around at the Monuments and different things atop this beautiful mountain, and it was cold up there. We had gone from the mid-to-high 80 degree temperatures when we started up the mountain, now the temperatures where in the high 60's. I had to put a jacket to take off the chill. As we looked around, I heard the voice of God say: "Go to the other side of the mountain." I looked around to see which one of my friends was playing some kind of sick trick on me, because the voice was loud and clear as if someone was standing right beside me commanding me to go. Now the guys I worked with were sharp! We were highly trained and were learned with various electronic devices, so I thought they had gotten together to play a trick on me. But, when I looked around, none were near me. Some were in the gift shop and others were checking the train out and looking at other monuments. So with great hesitation, I headed toward the backside of the mountain in an area where nobody else was. As I looked out at the view, I could see clearly, 68 miles north and the silhouette of the City of Denver. In between was Mountain tops, Valleys, Lakes, Rivers, and Roadways. The view was astonishing. I could see down at the base of Pikes Peak, a beautiful and vibrant blue lake that sat in the middle of the surrounding mountain chains. Then God spoke and said: "Frank, I'm sick and tired of dealing with boys. I WANT MY MEN BACK!" He said: "I'm not talking about little boys or kids, I'm talking about men (30 years or older), who are supposed to be mature men. It's time out for nonsense and foolishness! I'm sick and tired of all the games being played." At this point I was really apprehensive but I continued to listen and God continued by saying: "I'm choosing you because you have influence. You are known back at home in the community and from being a popular athlete. You are known nationally because you are one of the Poster Models for the FBI and many have seen you in the Magazines..." (From 1995 to 2005 I was featured in several major magazines representing the FBI. We were dubbed – "The FBI's Finest" and the advertisements highlighted the careers of different Special Agents. I was featured in Time, Life, Ebony, Black Enterprise, Ebony, Jet, Hispanic, and various College and Career Fair Journals). God continued to say: "I'm choosing you because you are not afraid. You have a voice and I know you will speak to My men." God finished this brief, one-way conversation, by stating: "You now see what is good... now go! Go, do my work!"

I was shook! Never had I ever had an experience like this! I had no idea what it was, but it was actually very scary. I remember the old saints quoting a phrase that: "You know when you know," but that didn't really explain to me what it was. I came to find out that the experience that I had with God on that mountain top on Aug. 22, 1197, was called a "Theophany" experience. THEOPHANY – is any direct, visual manifestation of the presence of God. The key word is visual, since God made His presence known and power known throughout the Bible in a variety of ways. But even in a theophany a person does not actually see God Himself, because that is an impossibility according to the scriptures (Exodus 33:20; 1 Timothy 6:16; and 1 John 4:12). What a person sees are God's unmediated presence. Moses, had a theophany experience when God took him on the backside of a mountain and showed him the burning bush. As Moses looked at the burning bush and God asked him to come closer to investigate, Moses realized that the bush while it was on fire, was not being consumed. There was nobody who could convince Moses that he was imagining or that he didn't really see what he thought that he saw, but this was a direct visitation from God. You best believe that he, as the old saints would say: "knew that he knew" he was in the presence of the Lord Almighty. When I stepped off that mountain and started my descent, you best believe I knew that I was in the presence of the Lord and I told no one. I simply responded to God, by saying: "YES LORD!" When we finally got to the bottom of the mountain. I got everybody out of the Tahoe and took a group photo with that beautiful lake in the background. I took the film of the entire trip to the store to get developed and when the pictures returned to me, this was the best shot of them all. It almost looked like a postcard. You have the crystal blue lake with the image of Pikes Peak in the background. Above the mountains are bountiful white and fluffy clouds. At the base of the mountain are several evergreen trees and between the lake and the base of the mountain is an ideal mirrored reflection of the clouds, mountains, and the trees. Clearly God was still speaking!

We got back in the Tahoe and headed back North for Denver. What an awesome day. It was a beautiful Friday and I didn't have to be back to work until that next evening. I had only six more days remaining on this S.O.R.T. trip. As we reported for duty the next evening it was "Wino" and I and we resumed our position in the alley off of 17th Street behind the Magnolia Hotel. As usual, at 12 midnight Sunday morning just like clockwork "Jimmy" appeared. "Wino" was in the driver's seat and I was in the passenger seat.

"Jimmy" came up to "Wino's" window smoking a cigarette and he was drunk. "Wino" engaged him in conversation as I sort of listened but concentrated on the activity going on across the street at the nightclubs. By the time I tuned back into their conversation I heard "Jimmy" say something about Jesus. As I recall, it wasn't anything big and he wasn't really concentrating on Jesus' name but he just said it as a figure of speech. No sooner had I heard him say Jesus' name, God said: "Frank do It!" I said in my mind: "Do what? I know You don't expect me to engage this dude about Christ right now! Besides, look at all these people out here right now. I don't know how he's going to react." God firmly instructed again: "DO IT!" Needless to say, I looked "Jimmy" square in the eyes and asked him: "Jimmy what did you just say? Did you say, Jesus?" Jimmy did not respond he kind of just looked at me blindly. So, I asked: "Jimmy are you afraid?" Still no response.

Here's the backdrop to all of this. Since 1995 I began studying Spiritual Warfare and absolutely fell in love with the study. I was so good at identifying what spirits to bind and to loose. I understood that everything you did had to be according to (Matthew 18:18) which declares: "I tell you the truth, whatever you bind on earth will be bound in heaven, and whatever you loose on earth will be loosed in heaven." I knew most of the Strongmen and could tell you what kind of fruit they had on their branches. I knew of the various Strongholds, understood how to identify demonic spirits and could call them out by their names. I was an expert in Spiritual Warfare "on paper..." but had never experienced it in my life. I understood the apostolic move of God and how it was supposed to operate but had no literal-hands on experience. God had prepared me for two years of intense study for what was about to come.

So I looked Jimmy square in the eyes again and said, "Jimmy, if you aren't afraid I dare you to say Jesus!"

He looked at me and in a quiet and unassuming and low tone voice began to say, "I AM THE GREAT I AM."

Okay, wow! So I asked him once again, I said, "Jimmy, if you are not afraid let me here you say Jesus!"

He did, he said it! He said, "Jesus."

I said, "Jimmy say it again." And he did. So I asked him to say it again and again, but the sixth time... I said, "Jimmy do you understand that there is *healing* in His Name?" I looked at him once more and said, "I dare you to say Jesus one more time Jimmy." He did, he said it one final time and I replied, "Jimmy do you understand that there is *power* in His Blood?" Oh my Goodness! Literally, all hell broke loose. All the movies I should not have watched when I was a little boy, *Rosemarie's Baby*, *The Omen*, *The Exorcist*, and *The Curse of Chucky*, all became very real to me...very quickly!

Jimmy's eyes became pierced, his voice deeply demonic, and he started approaching the front passenger side window where I was seated. As he was approaching my window from the front of the vehicle, his hand was motioning like he was cutting his throat.

He started frothing at the mouth and stuff was coming out of his eyes and nose as he was focused on me saying, "I'm gonna 'F*** in' kill you!" The stuff coming out of his mouth look like a clear bubbling foam. It was hedious.

When Jimmy got to the front panel of the passenger side corner of the vehicle, I placed my hand inside my vest on the butt of my gun and spoke to the spirit in an authoritative voice. I looked him square in the eyes but I wasn't talking to Jimmy, I was speaking directly to the diabolical spirit that was manifesting. I said, "You foul demonic spirit of rejection, fear, addiction, and yeah... strongman bondage, I bind you up right now, in the name of Jesus! I am a child of the King and covered by the Blood of Jesus! I loose the Spirit of Liberty and the Spirit of Adoption, right now in the name of Jesus!"

Jimmy stopped in his tracks, doubled over at the front corner panel of the vehicle and began to plead in his normal voice, "Please Frank, don't let the devil get me!" Because this was all new to me, I looked at Wino, and Wino looked back at me with a quizzical look, and before I could blink again I looked back at Jimmy. Well, this time Jimmy's voice was more vehement, his eyes were more pierced and the frothing was more intense. He had straightened back up and was headed directly toward me at the passenger side window. This time I didn't hesitate. I not only placed my hand on the butt of my gun, but I unsnapped the strap with my thumb. Now Jimmy was right outside of my window. It was hot outside and the windows were all the way down.

Then God spoke again, always teaching, he said, "The two things that you hate the most, I'm going to show you that they are very real." The two things that I was always very uneasy with was going to Church and having the Pastor call you out and prophesying to you. I was also very uncomfortable with anybody, ever, laying hands on me especially in the Church. My mindset was if you don't know me, don't even think about touching me.

God told me to take my hand off of my gun, snap it back and "do what I tell you to do." So I snapped my gun back into place all the while "Jimmy" is outside of my window threating to kill me. God said: "Lay hands on him and take your rightful authority." I stuck my right arm outside of the window and laid my hands on the top of "Jimmy's" head. I spoke to that vile spirit again and said: "Did you not hear what I said? I said I am a child of the King and covered by the blood of Jesus! You foul demonic spirit of Rejection, Fear, Addiction, and yes... STRONGMAN, Spirit of Bondage, I bind you up right now in the name of Jesus and I command you to flee! I loose the Spirit of Liberty and the Spirit of Adoption, right now in the name of Jesus!" At that point, "Jimmy" doubled over again and God said: "Now get of the vehicle and cover him and prophesy to his spirit!" So I jumped out of the vehicle and I'm a pretty decent sized dude, very athletic and squeezed this man like "nobody's business!" He was not getting lose and he certainly was going to sneak me. While squeezing him tight I began to prophesy to him. I first asked if he was saved and had he accept Jesus as his Lord and Savior. He said he had not, so I led him to Christ and he accepted. "Jimmy" was now saved! I then began to tell him that now he belonged to the Body of Christ and God was going to send him back to the shelter to bless others by his testimony, and how he would go on to lead others to Christ. The last thing I remember telling "Jimmy" as I held him tight was the following. I said: "Jimmy, I may never see you again, after today." I only had a few more days left there and as much as I fought coming on this trip, I now know why God had me here. It was never about the job, but about the personal and intimate experience with God." I loosened up my grip, gave "Jimmy" a hug and looked at him in the eyes and said: "Now, Go! To my amazement "Jimmy" left. It was only 12:30 am. "Jimmy" never left us before 6:00 am. But I instructed him to go and he did. To be very honest, I felt like Moses giving commands. LOL!

With ever great move of God, comes some sort of critique... even if it's internal. And I did, I immediately critiqued myself very harshly for on my first Spiritual Warfare experience. I called my wife that morning, excited about the events that had taken place early that morning. My wife began to just cry and we both prayed and thanked God for the elevation in the Spirit. Getting back to the critique, I gave myself an A+ on my obedience to God! I felt real good about that. Composure, I gave myself a B- on that because it was my first time and I didn't know what to expect. I gave myself a grade of a B+ on identifying the Stronghold and calling out the Strongmen that were in operation. For the laying on of hands and prophesying, I tapped out at a C- because this was very uncomfortable for me. However, there was one thing I absolutely believed I failed at, giving myself a straight up F. I was all over the Spirit of Bondage, Addiction and Fear. I could see all of those in operation and I went right to them. However, all the "Monday Morning Quarterbacking" and all the reflecting in the world still didn't answer why "Rejection" was the first thing that came out of my mouth as I was conducting Spiritual Warfare. I did not understand. I could not comprehend it and it bothered me. I only had three days left and would be heading back home. I remember prophetically telling "Jimmy" that I might never see him again but God was going to use how to be a mighty witness for Christ. That part was true because "Jimmy" never appeared again in the alley. I was happy, but still not satisfied because I didn't completely understand the entire Warfare process. To me, it had to make perfect sense. Frustrated with not seeing "Jimmy" anymore to check up on his progress, I demanded that "Wino" and I be granted the opportunity to work the front side of the Hotel on our last night. After all, we had worked the alley the whole time having to keep our "heads no a swivel." The front was easy, nobody bothered you and it was much less tense. On our last night there, "Wino" and I assumed a direct eye on the front of the hotel. Right around 12 midnight, "Wino" had gone out to use the restroom and I was in the driver's seat. It was another warm night and I had the windows down. A call come over the Bureau radio and said: "Uh, '1672?" (That was my call sign). I said: "1672 Copy, go ahead." They said: "Uh, your boy is here to see you." I quickly replied: "My boy? What boy? I don't have any boy's here! I don't know anybody in Denver." They advised that "Jimmy" was in the alley looking for me. With great anticipation I told them to send him around to the front and I immediately sat up in my seating waiting for him to turn the corner. After all, "Jimmy" was going to be all cleaned up. He wasn't going to have a stutter-step in his walk, and he surely wasn't going to smoking those stinking cigarettes. As "Jimmy" suddenly turned the corner I quickly became very disappointed. He was staggering as he walked toward me. He had on the same old raggedy clothes and he was smoking those dreadful cigarettes. When he came up to my driver's side window, I literally was about to punch him. That's how mad I was! It didn't help at all, the fact that he was blowing that stinking cigarette smoke in my face. As "Jimmy" talked I couldn't hear the words that were coming out of his mouth, that's how mad I was. In my mind I pleaded with God and said: "How God? How could you allow me to go through the entire Spiritual Warfare process and there is NO change? Why God? Why?"

The loving Daddy that He is to us, God allowed me to have my rant... then He gently put me in my place. I looked at "Jimmy" and flat out asked him the question I'd never asked him before. I said: "Jimmy why are you here? How did you get into this predicament?" "Jimmy" explained that he was 39 years old, had a 19 year old son living in Aurora that he had little-to-no contact with. He stated that he had a brother and sister that lived in Golden, CO, but didn't really talk to them. I look "Jimmy" squarely in the eyes again and told him that I was about to ask him a personal question and he didn't have to answer it if he didn't want to. He said okay, and I asked. I said: "Jimmy are your parents still alive." And just like any Spiritual Warfare manifestation, snot began to flow freely from his nose, he began to weep profusely, and gasp for air. (Spirits always exit from your orifices). It was almost like a baby who had just gotten beating. He was crying like a baby! This manifestation wasn't demonic but deep hurt and severe wounds were coming out. I'll never forget the words that "Jimmy" spoke to me next. He said: "Frank, ever since I can remember. Ever since I was yeah high, my Dad always called me a 'good for nothing.' A 'piss-ant.' He always called me an imbecile... he said I would NEVER AMOUT TO NOTHING." I'll tell you it was only a little after 12 midnight, but immediately after "Jimmy" said: "NEVER AMOUT TO NOTHING," he turned around and departed. He never said another word! He walked away down the block. I followed him with my eyes in my rear view mirror and the Lord spoke to me once again. He said: "Now, you have it... don't you ever doubt me again! I do everything well. The spirit of Rejection lead to the spirit of Fear; which in turn lead to the spirit of Addiction; finally leading up to the STRONGMAN – The Spirit of Bondage." This was truly a mind blowing experience and one, by which I would never question God again. Our shift was over at 7:00 am, so I went to use the restroom before we got on the road to head back to our hotel. I went downstairs to use the restroom in this beautiful and plush hotel. As I was relieving myself I was marveling at the amount of detail that was in the bathroom, marble floors and counters and the like. Then, Jesus spoke to me quoting the words He declared in (Matthew 10:32). He said: "Whoever acknowledges me before men, I will also acknowledge him before my Father in heaven. But whoever disowns me before men, I will disown him before my Father in heaven." I got back to my room and called my wife and advised her that God had "sealed the deal" and I was returning home "On Fire!" I now, truly understood why God took me clear across the Country to speak to me on the backside of a Mountain, and in order to have that supernatural Spiritual Warfare experience. I was excited to get back and begin the work that the Lord assigned my hands to do. We departed Denver on Thursday, August 28th on Fight #270 at 10:20 am Pacific Time and returned back in Philadelphia at 3:339 pm Eastern Time.

I prayed and meditated on the assignment that God had given me and nine months later, I finally garnered enough courage to execute what God instructed me back on that Mountain in 1997. On Saturday, May 2, 1998, we conducted our very 1st Spiritual Men of Warfare Visionaries (SMWV) meeting at my good friend's house. My friend, Co-worker (former FBI Agent), and mentor at the time, was none other than Mr. Calvin Poskey. Poskey was a jolly old soul. He was confident in who he was in Christ and was very influential. Poskey was on that trip to Denver in 1997 and I had shared my experience with him concerning the Call of God and what He desired. Poe agreed and hosted the first meeting, which consisted of thirteen men. I remember every man who attended. Thank you God for obedience!

6

"A SAFE PLACE TO LAND"

—⚬⚭⚬—

"Sometimes God allows us to cry, for tears to clear our eyes...
So we can clearly see the good things ahead."

Saturday, May 2, 1998 finally arrived and I was scared to death! I spent months praying and preparing for what I was going to say to all who attended our inaugural SMWV meeting. I have always been a very confident person, never one to really get nervous. However, when the hour had come and all had assembled in Poskey's house (7 pm), I was as nervous as "all get out!" My palms were sweaty, mouth as dry as cotton and I really could not focus. This was very different for me. What I would come to understand was that if I was totally confident in my own ability, then God was not leading it. It would have been all of me and none of God. What I know now, is that God was in total control of that meeting on that evening... all I did was duck and get out of his way! Let me explain.

In preparation for the meeting I had gone over and over a text from the book of Matthew (which I cannot remember to this day). I looked at the thirteen men, as they gazed back at me eagerly anticipating what I was about to say... and I said to them, "Open your Bibles to Matthew..." and again, I can't remember chapter nor verse. Whatever the text was, I turned to it and began to read. Two words into the reading I heard the Lord say: "SHUT THE BOOK!" Hmmmmmm? I've heard God speak before and I knew His voice, but I looked at the Bible then I looked back at the men... and I said to myself I'm not closing this book. So I attempted to read that very same chapter and verse again. Lo and behold, the same voice said: "I TOLD YOU TO SHUT THE BOOK!" I paused again, now this was very uncomfortable because the men were looking at me like, "what is this guy doing?" "Does he know what he's doing?" "Omg! Why did we even come here?" So, I tried to read it one more time. This time, in a very clear and authoritative voice, God said one final time: "I'M NOT GOING TO TELL YOU AGAIN… CLOSE THAT BOOK!" God went on to say to me: "What you have for these men, is not in that text… nor is it written in your notes. Begin to tell them your "real" testimony. This was unprecedented!

I detailed some of the events in my life that most of the men already knew. I came from a stable family, my mom and dad had been happily married for 37 years at that time. I didn't grow up in a rough neighborhood. I didn't have bouts with drugs and alcohol. I wasn't a troubled child and never had any run-ins with law enforcement. I was an All-Star athlete, a leader and presently was being featured in several National and International Magazines (Time, Life, Ebony, Essence, Black Enterprise, Hispanic, College Career & Planning, and Jet), as a poster model for the FBI. The one page advertisements read: "America's Finest… FBI Special People. Special Agents." The advertisement gave me a fake name and detailed my experiences as an FBI Agent. They knew I was a role model in the community and was readily available to help many causes. What they did not know was, that I was under a generational curse that no one could see. The thing that chased after me all my life and had caused me great pain, was the generational curse and strongman known as the Perverse Spirit.

The Bible speaks about the Perverse Spirit in (Isaiah 19:14). Some fruits of the Perverse Spirit are: pornography, sex, pre-marital sex, and contentiousness. In order to break that Spirit you have to bind the Perverse Spirit and Loose, God's Spirit; Pureness; and Holiness in its place. Let me explain in greater detail. According to spiritual warfare you have to close all "open doors" because sin is progressive. "Open doors" can include your lineage, ignorance, and can come through crisis in your life. As a matter of fact, an emotional or physical crisis may leave doors open that we have to go back and close so the enemy won't continue to torment us in that part of our lives.

The rules of engagement for spiritual warfare come from the scripture in (Matthew 18:18), where Jesus instructs: "Truly, I tell you, whatever you bind on earth will be bound in heaven, and whatever you loose on earth will be loosed in heaven."

So this Perverse Spirit was an "open door" in my life that need to be dealt with and closed! My testimony was that I started looking at pornography at a very young age. I had sex, way before I was ever supposed to. As a result had a child out of wedlock when I was barely 20 years old. Much of this behavior was learned by watching what my Daddy did. Was my Daddy a bad guy? Absolutely not! Until this day, he is my best friend and I love him dearly… but a generational curse was laid down on the men in our family. The sad thing about this was I now had three kids (two boys and a girl), and one more boy on the way. He would be born in 1998. So I had to deal with this curse and it would have to STOP with me so that my sons would now live under generational blessings. I decreed and declared all the binding and loosing necessary to receive the blessings of God for my family and this curse was now broken.

As I described in great detail all the struggle I had gone through as a result of this curse, the men in the meeting looked at me with compassion and empathy. Some readily identified with this spirit. The reputation of the person that stood before them was hard to separate from the image that was being described. The Bible says in (Revelation 12:11) that "we overcome him by the blood of the lamb and the word of our testimony." What my testimony did was to "open the doors & floodgates""and prepare a way of escape for the other men present. Each man began to detail his private struggles and disappointments. They began to speak very candidly about the things that had hurt and affected them during the course of their lives. Things nobody else knew! The ages of the men in the group varied. Some were in their late 50's, while the youngest were in their teens.

Immediately following all the testimonies and dynamic revelations, being obedient to God, I began to conduct spiritual warfare. I began binding and loosing whatever "Strongmen" I saw in operation. A "Strongman" is simply a demonic stronghold. From these "Strongmen" you can have various fruits from that tree. For instance, one of the "Strongmen" is the Spirit of Jealousy. Some fruits of the Spirit of Jealousy include: murder, hatred, cruelty, division, envy, anger, rage, and extreme competition." There are sixteen "Strongholds" that we deal with in the spirit realm and they are: Spirit of Division; Familiar Spirit; Spirit of Jealousy; Lying Spirit; Perverse Spirit; Spirit of Pride (Haughtiness); Spirit of Heaviness; Spirit of Whoredoms; Spirit of Infirmity; Dumb and Deaf Spirit; Spirit of Bondage; Spirit of Fear; Seducing Spirits; Spirit of Anti-Christ; Spirit of Error, and the Spirit of Death.

Our very first SMWV meeting began at 7 pm that night and we did not conclude until almost 2 am in the morning, because the brothers had a lot they needed to get out! We chased many demons out of that place on that evening, but moreover, men where healed; delivered; and set free of demonic oppression. The last thing I told those men on that evening before we departed was this: If you think that you will use tonight's forum as a sounding board for gossip tomorrow or any other time in the future... you mouth will not open! God will not allow you to utilize for gossip, what was used to set each of you free tonight. I decree and declare that this place, this forum (SMWV meeting) will be a SAFE PLACE FOR MEN TO LAND. It will be a place where they can unload all of their baggage and not be judged or looked a strangely.

7

EYES ARE WINDOW TO THE SOUL

*"Don't miss out on a blessing just because it is not packaged
the way you expected!"*

As a FBI Agent, one of my most memorable cases occurred early on in my career. It was early in 1999, when my partner and I (Fran Ford) were assigned to a "Cold-Case" Homicide. Fran, God love his soul, was my favorite partner of all-time. He and I were sort of the "Odd-Couple." I was a young, black male, new generation (hip-hop type) FBI Agent. Fran, on the other hand, was an older white male, cigar smoking, deep voice, nearing the end of his career, Philadelphia Police Officer. He was assigned to our Task Force and had done tremendous work the Philadelphia Police Department Homicide Division.

Fran was very methodical and things had to be done just the way he liked it. I'll never forget, it was in the dead of winter (one of the coldest days), as we hit the street and departed our garage… Fran lit up that horrible cigar of his. I hate Cigars and Cigarette smoke – as previously mentioned. As we arrived at street level, Fran rolled down the two front windows in our vehicle and motioned me to "shush!" I said, "Huh? Freddy what are you doing?" He advised that I should be quiet because he had to "hear the Streets." Needless to say, I began a very quick and humble prayer right on the spot because I had no idea what I was dealing with. Lord, help me to hold out!

Anyway, Fran and I were instructed to go and interview a particular person about a Cold-Case homicide that occurred in a bad part of the City. We arrived at the assigned residence and identified ourselves properly, myself with the FBI and Freddy with the Philadelphia Police Department. After a lengthy interview with the residents it was later determined that not much was known about the homicide. However, they could lead us to someone else who had more detailed information regarding the incident. Fran and I agreed to speak with that person, but the residents were very cautious and stated that they would have to speak with that particular individual first because they did not like cops. They further advised that this individual had recently been released from prison and was very angry, so they had to make sure it was okay for us to speak with them. Finally, they warned that they could not be responsible for the actions of this person because, at any moment, this individual could snap. According to them, it was not unusual for this individual to assault (fight, stab, or shoot) law enforcement officers.

The meeting was finally arranged. At the table was Fran and I, along with the two individuals we had originally interviewed concerning this homicide. A short time later they introduced us to the individual who could provide us with more information. Immediately that individual sat down at the table with all of us and busted out laughing! The individual look very rugged. They had on a bandana on their head and wore very dark sunglasses. The individual looked at Fran and I and said, "Ya'll ain't no FBI! Get the F#*% outta here!" Fran jumped in immediately with that authoritative voice of his and said, "Now listen here!" In my mind, I'm saying, "God please help us because it's about to get REAL UGLY-REAL FAST up in this place." The individual became immediately agitated and started cussing and fussing exclaiming their disdain for law enforcement. Before it escalated any further, I looked at the two original individuals and asked if I could speak with person, alone? Fran glanced at me with a quizzical look, so did the two individuals. I asked them all to step outside and let me speak to the individual alone. Cautiously, they agreed.

While things were beginning to escalate, I had noticed a young child's picture on a mantle in the room. So I (now alone with the person) looked at the individual in the eyes (or what I could see), and asked very nicely if they could remove their sunglasses. Not so graciously, that individual asked me why (with several expletives) they had to remove their glasses. I stood my ground and asked that they please remove them. Reluctantly, the individual slowly took off their glasses. Behind those dark glasses were eyes that had rage and anger in them. The individual's eyes were bloodshot red and puffy, it appeared that the person had been crying. At that point, not the Agent... but the Man of God stared deeply into their eyes and said: "Did you know that the eyes are the window to your soul?" I told them that I heard all the angry words and tough talk they were spewing... but deep down on the inside I saw a wounded and hurt little individual. Immediately, that person began to breakdown and cry profusely.

I asked if the child in the picture was theirs and they said, "Yes." As we continued to converse, I let them know that I knew what it was like to grow up in the city and under-stood the "Street Rules." But, I posed this question to them... I said, "What if your baby was shot and killed today and somebody witnessed it but never gave the information regarding the shooting, how would you feel?"

God was showing me even back then, it was one thing to be an Agent… but it was another thing to be a Man of God with discernment. I knew very clearly on that day that being an FBI Agent was what I did… it was not who I was. I was a "Spiritual Sniper" for the Lord. I hope that makes sense to someone. What I am trying to relay is that on that day, God clearly defined who I was in Him. He showed me that my success and path in the Bureau would be different from other Agents.

As a result of allowing God to use me in such a powerful fashion, that two-year Cold-Case homicide was solved in two months. And to this day, that individual and I remain in constant contact for the building and uplifting of the Kingdom of God. Just think, if I simply stereotyped this individual (as so many others had done), I would have missed out on an opportunity and blessing because I would have just focused on the package it came in. There is an old adage that says you can't judge a book by its cover… I'm so glad that God allowed me to open that book up and discover the awesome contents it contained.

8

THE 1996 OLYMPICS – ATLANTA

—⟋⟍⟍—

"When God is ready for us to move forward and we resist,
He will moves us by any means necessary."

In the summer of 1996 I had the opportunity of a lifetime with the FBI. I was assigned to work the Summer Olympics which were help in Atlanta, GA. What an honor this was! I and five other members from my elite team were awarded the opportunity to work and be a part of this festive event. For me, it was a once-in a-lifetime opportunity. On July 13, 2006, we got into our cars and headed south to Atlanta. We departed at 9:00 am, all bright-eyed and bushy tailed and just super-excited to be heading down to the Olympics. However, when we reached North Carolina we ran into Hurricane Bertha. Oh my God! I have driven in many parts of this Country under many conditions and I would like to think of myself as a very experienced driver, but driving through this hurricane presented many challenges. According to good old Wikipedia regarding Bertha:

"North Carolina bore the brunt of the hurricane in the United States. Storm surges destroyed several fishing piers, marinas, and boats. A combination of storm surge and strong winds damaged over 5,000 homes and buildings with at least four destroyed. There were two deaths in the state."

It was very challenging for all of us to navigate through this hurricane. As we travelled through Charlotte, NC, visibility was less than a cars length. But we pressed on and arrived at our destination (Stockbridge, GA) at approximately 8:30 pm. Several days before the Olympics began, we all were sworn in and received our Peace Officer status with the GBI (Georgia Bureau of Investigation). We also received our official Olympic Credentials. The 1996 Olympics began on July 19 and ended on August 4.

During this S.O.R.T. trip, I had the opportunity to meet several Agents and Support Staff that worked in the Atlanta Division. Within the first few days in Atlanta, I met a very special young lady by the name of Brenda Baines. Brenda was a very quiet, polite and well and respected young lady who worked on the Professional Support Staff side of the FBI. One thing that was quickly evident, Ms. Brenda was known as "The Church Lady" in the Office. Okay God, what are You trying to tell me now, I asked myself. I arrived in Atlanta and meet this very nice person and we so many things in common, yet we are very different. What is this connection? Is it a connection at all? Needless to say, I had the opportunity to minister some things to Ms. Brenda... but she also spoke very richly into my life concerning the things that God had in store for me. I just could not shake it! No matter where I was assigned, Los Angeles; Compton; Crenshaw; Hollywood; Tucson; Phoenix; Jacksonville; Charlotte; Chicago; Boston; Columbia S.C.; Albany; Buffalo, NYC (all five Boroughs); Richmond; Nashville; Birmingham; Dallas; Denver; Colorado Springs; or Salt Lake City... God always sent someone to speak to me concerning His message of the God News of the Gospel of Jesus Christ!

On July 18, I had the opportunity to brush shoulders with Kirk Franklin & the Family (I sat right next to him and his new wife, Tammy), Jonathan Butler, Najee, and Will Downing at the illustrious House of Blues – 213 Luckie St, Atlanta, GA.

Interesting fact is that this venue was opened up days before the 1996 Olympics began and this was the opening night. Little did I know that I would reconnect with Kirk Franklin much later on down the line? God granted me to assist with Kirk's Executive Protection detail, in November of 2011. On November 25 of that Year, I escorted and secured Kirk to Philadelphia's Gospel radio station Praise 103.9 fm. He was interviewed regarding his upcoming "Hello Fear" concert that evening at Sharon Baptist in Philly, where Bishop Keith Reed is the Senior Pastor. I got the opportunity to grace the stage and serve, Kirk, Isaac Carree, Amber Bullock, Deon Kipping and Jason Nelson, behind the scenes that evening.

Kirk is a very humble and gracious individual. After the concert was over he spent hours making sure he signed ever autograph of his fans, old and young. When Kirk was finally done (approximately 1:00 am – he is very dedicated to his craft), I was responsible for safely returning him to his Hotel.

***SIDE NOTE ABOUT KIRK FRANKLIN:

After all was said and done for the evening, the concert was over and all folk were greeted... I went to my vehicle in preparation for Kirk's departure. I wanted to make sure that everything was fine for him. Car warmed up... Check! Heat just right... Check! Now, for the music, maybe some Jazz? Nope! I put him the "Hello Fear" CD, after all, I couldn't go wrong with this. Kirk got in the car and softly said: "Hey Apostle, I can't deal with that Kirk Franklin dude. Please turn him off." Hilarious! I'm still cracking up over that experience as I write this today!

I know I'm jumping around a bit (from the past to the present), but I'm just putting it all down as it comes to me. Believe me, I'm not scatter-brained, but I want you to get this as God is giving it to me. So please bear with me, okay?

Back to the 1996 Olympics... finally, I was introduced to Will by a good friend of mine and FBI Agent, Jack Robbins (New York and now Phoenix Division).

"Okay God... I hear you loud and clear! Yes, I will tell them!" So, being obedient to God, this building was founded in 1898 and was originally a Baptist Temple. Shortly after the Olympics was over, the House of Blues went out of business and the name of the present location is – The Tabernacle or the "The Tabby."

TRAGEDY! On July 27, 1996, a terrorist bomb attack erupted on Centennial Olympic Park. I was in the park at the time and the blast, a pipe bomb contained in a backpack, killed one female and injured 111 people. Another, Turkish cameraman died of a heart attack. I along with groups of surveillance team members were assigned to keep a close watch on (then subject), Richard Jewell. I eventually went undercover at the apartment complex he lived in, acting as a resident to get a poolside view of his activities. We later found out that Eric Robert Rudolph was the perpetrator of the devastating bombing.

9

"I SURVIVED MY HATE CRIME"

—⟡—

"Your passion is important to your purpose!"

As a FBI Agent, Negotiator and Employee Assistant Program (EAP Coordinator) for the FBI, I was very passionate about people. My passion for others was crucial to my purpose in the Bureau. God created me to assist others and to give it my all in doing so.

On October 3, 2006, I was assigned to a potential hate crime case. The initial information received was that a lady who worked at the Philadelphia Sheraton Suites Airport hotel had just received a hate note. I was given orders to go investigate. When I arrived at the hotel I asked for Mrs. Nina Timani, who was the Director of Sales for the hotel and the victim. Mrs. Timani is a Muslim Arabic American who is originally from Egypt. One day prior, she received an envelope in her inbox on the outside of her office door that read:

"Remember 9/11, You and your kids we'll tie to the fence and die."

Other words contained in this note included: "Realize the Power," "Pay," "Religion in the 20th Century," Most Notorious Criminals," and the words "Strategically Planned" with a written arrow leading to the word, "Death."

When I arrived at the hotel I carefully examined the note. It was evident that someone from the inside... someone who had access to her office had carefully crafted this note using some sort of brochure clippings. The person responsible for this note had cut out clippings (all different type settings) and pasted them on this neatly folded

8 x 10 piece of white paper. The perpetrator placed this note in a small mailing envelope, wrote "Nina Timani" on the outside and placed it in her inner office box.

Being a FBI Agent, my job required me to travel quite a bit and I was used to staying in various hotels. So I immediately asked Mrs. Timani where the brochure rack was. She directed me to a place that was sort of out-of-the-way, located near swimming pool in the back of the hotel. I quickly scanned the various brochures and immediately made eye contact with the initial threat in the threat letter, "REMEMBER 9/11." From there, I examined every brochure in the rack from cover to cover and discovered that all the wording in the threat letter came from several of the brochures contained in the rack. I immediately told Mrs. Timani that someone on the inside and one who had access to her office was the culprit.

Mrs. Timani gave me a list of approximately 60 people (sales associates, maintenance personnel, front desk employees, restaurant employees and general contractors) who she thought had that type of access. When asked if there was any person that would be her enemy, Timani said she could not think of anyone. For days, I interviewed each person. At the completion of the interviewing process (approximately a week and a half) technically I was at a loss. Of all the people I had interviewed, nobody seemed to stand out as a prime suspect. At this point I could have simply taken the attitude that this is impossible to figure out and tossed the case aside. But there was something! Something just did not sit right with my spirit. Hmmmmmmmmmmmm! Have you ever had that feeling?

I went home, prayed, and asked God to give me the wisdom and discernment of King Solomon in the Bible. I wanted to be able to effectively judge who was being truthful and who was not. So I continued to pray. After praying, replaying each interviewee in my mind and carefully reviewing my notes, I saw a few people who clearly seemed a bit nervous. They tried to play cool, calm and collected... but I was a veteran investigator. I was an experienced interrogator and effective hostage negotiator. Surely, I could discern if someone was lying to me. "A DIFFERENT WAY," were the words that stuck in my spirit. I had to have a different approach. So I returned to the hotel weeks later with a different strategy.

I re-interviewed approximately 10 people with one specific person in my focus. This time, I admonished each person to remember that if you lie to a Federal Agent you could be arrested for that violation, alone (18 U.S. Code –Section 1001). Each person stuck to what they had previously said, but the one I was focusing on seemed to go out of their way to assist and flatter me. They seemed overly concerned. But to my investigative eye they were masking something by trying to over compensate. So I concluded my second round of interviews and said thank you to each, but I still had nothing concrete.

One week later I received a call from an attorney who said that his client, one of the 10 I had re-interviewed wanted to provide me with information regarding the hate crime case. Long –story-short, I met with the attorney and his client and I received all the information necessary to get a warrant for the perpetrator's arrest. The perpetrator was female who worked closely with Mrs. Timani. She was a Supervisor for Mrs. Timani and was not pleased with her management style so she wanted to intimidate Mrs. Timani. The perpetrator (who is documented in public records regarding this case, but one whose name I will not publish out of respect and common courtesy) had come up with three different scenarios to get to Mrs. Timani. One was to simply walk up to her and punch her the face. Second, was to flatten all four of her car tires. And the third, was to concoct this threat letter. The latter choice is what the perpetrator decided to use.

On March 6, 2007 myself and another FBI Agent went to the Sheraton Suites Airport Hotel and arrested the perpetrator. At their guilty plea on June 22, 2007, the perpetrator admitted to committing to a federal hate crime by sending a note threating violence to her boss at work, who was an Arab and Muslim American in attempt to interfere with Mrs. Timani's federally protected employment activity. It was proven in court that during the early morning hours of Monday, October 2, 2006, the perpetrator left an anonymous threating letter in her Mrs. Timani's office at the hotel. The perpetrator had affixed words and phrases which were cut from publications and brochures including the phrases "REMEMBER 9/11."

"These attacks against individuals because of their race, ethnicity, or religion are contemptible, un-American, and will not be tolerated," said Acting Assistant Attorney General Rena J. Comisac.

This case was investigated by the Philadelphia Field Office of the FBI (me being the case agent) and was prosecuted by Assistant U.S. Attorneys Micky Swann and Joe White and Civil Rights Division Trial Attorney Eric L. Gibson. This case was a trend setter and set a precedent in the Eastern District of Pennsylvania (EDPA). In a news release issued from Washington, D.C. on October 24, 2007, the Justice Department said the conviction was the 34th for a federal bias crime against a Muslim, an Arab, a Sikh or a South Asian since the September 11, 2001 attacks. It was the first in the Eastern District of Pennsylvania.

It was a rare case of a federally prosecuted hate crime and the Justice Department sought the maximum penalty (a yearlong prison sentence for the misdemeanor charge). District Court Judge, Gene Pratter also sentenced the perpetrator to 200 hours of community service at a local mosque. Mrs. Timani and the perpetrator faced each other during a tear-filled hour hearing.

"You might ask... why make a federal case of this," Judge Pratter said. "Because our society cannot afford to dismiss this kind of conduct. This is a very serious crime. There is an incendiary quality to this," Pratter added. Special Assistant U.S. Attorney Eric L. Gibson stated: "There are just some things you don't do. Racism is contagious." Finally, Mrs. Timani cried in the courtroom and let the people know that she was surprised to learn that the perpetrator sent the note. Mrs. Timani said the two had been friends and although work had been stressful she would have never believed the perpetrator would resort to this. Mrs. Timani said that at one point, the perpetrator watched her children.

"In my community, we don't like to go to the FBI. But Special Agent Frank Burton Jr., was different. The FBI should be proud to have people like Agent Burton in its organization," Mrs. Timani said.

Today that very hate crime remains on the FBI's website as a public service announcement. It is presented in video format and is complete with Mrs. Timani's transcript. It can be found at:

http://www.fbi.gov/news/videos/i-survived-my-hate-crime

10

THE PERFECT SEASON

———<>———

"BORDERLINE PERFECTION"

"PERFECTION" – without flaw, or error, a state of completion or fulfillment.

This is the final chapter of my book. How ironic it serves as the eleventh part of my book and the tenth chapter. The number eleven is spiritual symbolic of: "Last-Stop, Finish," or the "Ending" of something. The number ten signifies *(MEASURE)* – trial, test or temptation. Wow! Look at God! I told you how He is the perfect orchestrator.

God's perfection means that He is complete in Himself. He lacks nothing. He has no flaws. By contrast, Human Perfection is relative and dependent on God for its existence. Because perfection in this life... on this side of glory, is never reached, people will continue to sin. (Philippians 3:12) states this theory best when the Apostle Paul writes: "Not that I have already obtained all this, or have already arrived at my goal, but I press on to take hold of that for which Christ Jesus took hold of me... Forgetting what is behind and straining toward what is ahead. I press on toward the goal to win the prize for which God has called me heavenward in Christ Jesus." And (1 Thessalonians 5:23) reminds us, "May God Himself, the God of peace, sanctify you through and through. May your whole spirit, soul and body be kept blameless at the coming of our Lord Jesus Christ?"

God called me to reflect on how I was to put this book together and had me confront the question: "Why would it take me an entire year to finish it?" Let me share my process with you.

As soon as I retired from the FBI (December 31, 2013), I started out writing with such excitement and much zeal to share with you my journey. I "flew out of the blocks" and was moving quickly, "full-steam-ahead." But I was interrupted. I said, I'm sorry God. Excuse me? What did you say? God spoke to me two-thirds of the way of finishing this book, He simply said: "SLOW." And for the life of me I could not understand why I, a person who was never at a loss for words, could not put anything on paper.

God reassured me and softly said, "Just watch what I am doing. I promise it will make perfect sense in the end." As a result, it does! It is crystal-clear to me now. God demonstrated this experience through my two youngest sons, Frank and Zachariah. We call him Zach. God was putting through a test.

In May of 2014, Frank and Zach's, Varsity High School Football Team, William Penn High School (WPHS) in New Castle, DE started out on a quest. From the very 1st day of 7-on-7 drills with twelve Delaware High Schools participating, the WPHS football team starting talking about being State Champions. The starting date of the football camp was May 27, 2014 and Middletown High School was the Camp's host.

Led by Head Coach, Marvin Dooley, the football team didn't get to display much because for the first four days it thunder stormed. However, on the final day of the camp, Saturday, May 31, skies were clear and all teams got to compete in 7-on-7 drills. WPHS faired very well against all the teams they went up against. At the completion of the camp as they were walking off the field, many of the State's Football Teams looked at the WPHS and began to encourage, "Yo, ya'll gonna win the Chip!" For those who don't understand, it means that they believed WPHS was going to win the Delaware State Football Championship.

From June to August the WPHS team dedicated themselves to strenuous weight training weekly. There were over 65 dedicated young men who showed up every week to improve in the weight room. When August arrived the team went through the dreaded "three-a-days!" This is where the kids arrived early in the morning (practicing three times in that day) and not return home until it was dark outside. Many "old-timers" who played football remember how tough these practices where. For those of you who have never played football, let me just tell you that these practices are brutal. This period of a couple of weeks is known as the pre-season.

After pre-season practices, it was time to be tested to see how the team faired. So WPHS scheduled three scrimmage games against: Dover, Penns Grove (NJ), and Smyrna High Schools. Things look promising as the Offense started to look alive and the Defense looked like it was beginning to gel. Still there was much work to be done. It was evident that at the end of these scrimmage games that this football team was starting to become cohesive and looking for an identity.

Let me digress for a brief moment. In 2012 WPHS went 3-7 and was a virtual laughing stock. WPHS historically has been a team that was respected and at times, even feared. However, for whatever reasons, they fell from grace. In 2012, Frank was a freshman and played on the Varsity team. In 2013, Coach Dooley took the reigns as Head Coach of WPHS School and he began to return the glory back to the team. In Coach Dooley's first year, WPHS went 7-4 and earned a trip to the State Championship Playoffs. They lost in the 1st round to Caesar Rodney High School. They were only two games away from competing for the State Championship. I will never forget the taste that loss left in the players mouths. Frank was now a sophomore and starting Tight End, he also played a considerable amount of time at Defensive End. Zach only a freshman, was the backup Quarterback and saw time as the holder on extra points. WPHS players knew that they had worked hard during the season but just did not finish well. They vowed to return to the playoffs in 2014.

Back to the beginning of the 2014 regular season. If WPHS was to return to the Playoffs, they had a heck of a test in front of them. The Season began on September 6 and right "out-of the-gate," on the schedule was the two best teams in the State. WPHS easily defeated St. Mark's 24-0. The following week, they defeated perennial great, Salesianum High School. It was a hard fought battle, but in the end, WPHS was victorious. The score was 16-10. WPHS was 2-0 and after defeating the two best teams in the State (despite being picked as favorites for the Season), still did not get the respect they deserved from local sports writers and others. However, they had something the others did not... "A Single Focus." They vowed not to let anything deter them from their purpose. Their purpose was to win the State Championship.

In the next four games, WPHS defeated the following teams: A.I. DuPont (56-23), Appoquinimink (44-0), Newark (51-15), and Middletown (21-7). By now WPHS was a solid 6-0 and enroute to the "Chip." But, I believed that they needed something more.

I knew many of the young men on the team because I had either coached them in some sport when they were younger... or I just spent a lot of time around all the sports teams encouraging the youth. I was always at the school because Frank and Zach both play Football, Basketball, and Baseball. Not only did I already have a good rapport with the kids and their parents, I was beginning to have a rapport with Coach Dooley. So I approached Coach Dooley and asked him after the Middletown game, if he and his team was amenable to attending a Church Service on the following Sunday. God placed it on my heart to invite the football players, coaches, cheerleaders, parents, students, administration, and school board leaders to attend this special service.

This is the vision God gave me. Our church, Perfect Will Ministries is in the same community WPHS is located. How awesome would it be for the Church and the Community to come together to worship, honor each other and fellowship? Now, I understood that everyone was not Christian and some would not attend, but I also understood that there were many of the players, coaches, and individuals who were Christians, would appreciate the invite. Reflecting back as I think about it… if I did this on my own without consideration and prayer, this would be risky. It would be risky because everyone could have rejected the idea. It was a very delicate situation because the people and coaches could have said no and looked at my boys in a different light. What I did not want to do was come up with some notion that I just wanted to do, then have my boys suffer the consequences.

Just like the vision God gave me for PWM, this vision was a "God Vision." You may ask, "Apostle what exactly is a God Vision?" A God Vision can only be accomplished through opportunistic faith that views: Obstacles as Opportunities and turns Defeats into Victories. That's it, right there! If God is in it, then there is no limit! I knew God was all in the underpinnings of this Vision.

I went all out for these young men and their school community. Based on my previous experience as a Media Representative with the FBI, I sent out a Media Advisory to all media outlets in the area. I informed them of the accomplishment of this team, their National Rank at the time (945 in the Country at the time), and I gave the WPHS Football team a name. I gave them an identity. In the Media Advisory I called them "The Band of Brothers." "The Band of Brothers" was a group of young men from various backgrounds, socio-economic status and multiple races, all who came together for one cause. To win! And these "Band of Brothers" were led by one General, Coach Dooley.

On Sunday, October 12, 2014, WHPS landed on PWM. I deemed this Sunday, "William Penn High School Team Appreciation/Jersey Day." I the team wear their football jerseys and our entire congregation dressed down and wore their favorite sports team jersey. Because God was in the details the turnout of players, coaches, students and members of the community was phenomenal. A major T.V. news station called and advised me that they would attend the Service to report on it and recognize the Team's efforts. I preached an encouraging word and gave each person present, keys of how to win in Life and how to stay focused.

The Blessing behind all of this resulted when I conducted the altar call. When I finished preaching on that day, over 40-some players, coaches and members of the community responded to the call. That means these individuals got out of their seats and walked up to the Church's altar. Some gave their lives to Jesus Christ and were saved, others who were back-slidden, repented for their sins. Yet, others simply requested prayer to stay focused and complete whatever task or assignment God had them on. All the Angels in Heaven were rejoicing on this day!

The following week, WPHS played there toughest game of the season against Concord High School. This game served as the very first time in WPHS' history that they would play in a night game at their stadium. It was also a game that would honor Breast Cancer

Survivors and bring attention to those who lost the battle to this disease. Lights were rented and brought in for this special event. Moreover, WPHS now had a "bull's-eye" on their backs. Everybody wanted to beat this undefeated giant. We defeated Concord in a very physical game. The final score was 28-21. Concord was a very formidable foe.

WPHS finished out the regular season with three victories over Charter (43-16), Glasgow (35-0) and Charter (55-0). Our regular season record was 10-0, but we still received no respect from Delaware Media. We were #1 Seed in Division I of the State Tournament and now ranked approximately 550 in the Nation. Yet, in the local newspaper we were picked to lose to St. Mark's (a team that we had previously defeated 24-0 in the first week of the Season). The writer said that we had not faced a quarterback like theirs before. This particular QB was lighting up the State with impressive numbers and was injured when we first played them. What people outside of WPHS did not know was that these "Band of Brothers" had taken it a step further. They had nicknamed the Defense the "Brigade" and "Hit-Squad." The Offense, not to be left out, selected the Military name – the "Arsenal." St. Marks had a QB that WPHS had not seen, but WPHS had some artillery that St. Marks could have never imagined.

On November 22, 2014 WPHS faced off with St. Marks in the Semi-Finals of the State Championship. Coach Dooley blessed me with the opportunity to be the pre-game motivational speaker. One significant note was that Coach Dooley's Mother had passed days before this pivotal game. I would like to take this brief moment to honor Mrs. Sue Ann (Watts) Dooley. Many who knew her intimately called her "Snookie." Rest in peace, Mom Dooley. This is my dedication to you.

Coach Dooley was very close to his mother and privately mourned, yet he maintained focus in order to complete this task. The WPHS players actually gained momentum by watching the Coach's strength in adversity. Yet, not a word was mentioned about this in the newspaper. All the media talked about was how probable WPHS was going to lose because of the opposing QB. WPHS had home-field advantage and defeated St. Marks in this game with a robust score of 42-14.

Finally, realizing we had a good thing going, Coach Dooley asked me to serve as the WPHS Football Team Chaplain. He asked me if I didn't mind speaking to the Team before the State Championship game. I agreed. On Saturday, November 29, 2014, I gave the pre-game motivational speech to this awesome group of young men. I could see it in their eyes that they were focused and really wanted to win it. Each player appeared to be "All-In!" I advised them that they deserved to be on this stage. I reminded them of all the hard work they had put in to get to this point. And finally, I admonished them that "BIG PLAYERS" show-up in Big Games! That was the key phrase I left them with… "BIG PLAYERS!" I told them that every time they got tired and wanted to quit, somebody needed to yell: "BIG PLAYERS!" I told them that if a player fumbled, dropped a pass, or missed a tackle... I told them not to get down on that player and begin to criticize each other but yell: "BIG PLAYERS!" I let them know that out of all the months, days, and weeks, of hard work they put into this Season... if they would just sacrifice 60 more minutes on this day to winning one more time, then they would achieve something very special. They would have at their disposal something very unique. Something not everybody could not be able to talk about. Not only would they be State Champs, but they would have embarked on "The Perfect Season," 12-0. Wow! What an opportunity! I advised them that they were really playing for "Legacy." Years after this day was over, it would be a day that would live on in infamy. They would talk about this day for the rest of their lives and their children's, children, children would talk about this incredible Year.

As I finish, I want you to experience God's awesomeness. I want you to see spiritually how He does everything and does all things well.

In (Ecclesiastes 7:8), the Bible says: "The END of a thing is better than its beginning." On this 29th day of November, WPHS found itself right back where it had started on May 27. This whole journey started, if you remember, on that date at Middletown High School. All teams had one vision, one goal... to win the State Championship. Lo and behold, WPHS was facing Middletown High School in the State's biggest game of the season. Thousands of fans made their way to the University of Delaware Stadium to attend this game. And yup, you guessed it... in spite of everything the WPHS team had gone through they were picked to lose. None of that mattered, however, because they understood that "the door that God opened, no man could shut." So, as a team, the collectively decided to "Praise God in the hallway!" Somebody knows what that means! It means that while you are waiting for your blessing to manifest and before God opens that particular door for you, you just praise Him in the hallway! Hallelujah!

The Newspaper headlines talked about how Middletown would beat WPHS because of the "two-headed" running backs they had. But we had the best running backs in the State. We had the best Tight End, Defensive and Offensive Lines in the State, as well. They talked about how Middletown's Coach had been in the last four State Championship games and how his experience would allow his team to overcome WPHS' talent. Plus, WPHS could never do it again. They could not beat another team they had already defeated in the regular season. No way could they do it twice in a row! That would be like catching lightning in a bottle. By all accounts, according to the newspapers, Middletown was already handed the Championship Trophy. The problem was... they still had to play the game. Theories were all good, but the Sports Writers were not going to play this game.

When the smoke settled and all the dust was cleared, WPHS defeated Middletown 42-17. It was the same exact score as the Semi-Final game. What was the significance of this score? Symbolically, what did it mean? Forty and Two. The number 40 is symbolic of a Generation (Legacy). It is sometime symbolic of Probation (God's people spent 40 years in the desert, a period of probation, until all the undesirables were killed off so the rest could proceed to the Promised Land). WPHS was setting up a legacy and generations after would talk about this awesome feat. The number 2 is symbolic of: Dividing, Discerning, Judging, or Separating. God was separating WPHS from the rest of the pack. In a sense, He was separating the "wheat from the tares." You know this saying: "The cream always rises to the top."

The number 17 is associated with: Incompletion, Immaturity, and being Undeveloped. God was putting a mark of completion on WPHS' Season. Okay, yup... I got it God! I hear you loud and clear now. WPHS finished number 241 in the Country and number 1 in the State of Delaware. The "Brigade," WPHS' defense only gave up 92 points in 12 games, allowing only 9.2 points a game. The "Arsenal," WPHS' offense scored over 373 points over those 12 games. Thanks incredible, ya'll!

HERE'S THE LESSON: Nothing is "Perfect" unless God is in it. Secondly: Just like the WPHS Football Team started out back in May of 2014 – You have got to have a VISION. (Proverbs 29:18) tells us, "Without a vision, a people perish." They set a goal and worked toward accomplishing it. Third: Never become anxious in what God has given you, just stay focused and rely on the peace of God. (Philippians 4:6-7) reminds us, "Do not be anxious about anything, but in every situation, by prayer and petition, with thanksgiving, present your requests to God. And the peace of God, which passes all understanding, will guard your hearts and your minds in Christ Jesus." Fourth: You have got to persevere in spite of adversity. After losing his mother, Coach Dooley demonstrated to these young men of how to endure hardship and pain, yet accomplish the goal that God sets before you. It showed me that even though God tells us He knows the plan He has for us. Plans to prosper and get us to an expected end, it is not always smooth and easy... but it is always true. (2 Corinthians 4:8-10) encourages us, "We are hard pressed on every side, but not crushed; perplexed but not in despair; persecuted, but not abandoned; struck down, but not destroyed. We always carry around in our body the death of Jesus, so that the life of Christ may be revealed in our body." And finally, this WPHS team and the complete season taught us all, how to finish and win. This is described, as earlier stated in (Philippians 3:12). This Season taught us all what a thousand sermons ever could. Thanks for making me wait God. My strength is renewed and I'm wiser because of it. While we can never be "Perfect" on this side of glory, this is what I call "Borderline Perfection."

FINAL THOUGHTS

If you were looking to this book to discover some sophisticated FBI techniques, I'm sorry! Like a melting pot, this book is a consortium (a mosaic & a perfect blend) of my life's experiences and how God got me to where I am spiritually. Much of what I have done in my personally life and in the FBI, was never of my own accord. I have been recognized as the "Best" in many facets of my life, "America's Finest," and even called an "Expert." But God takes preeminence over all. He is the "Wind beneath my wings" and the reason why I've been able to soar. He is everything to me!

This book is a testament to what real service is about. The Bible tells us in (Mark 10:43), "Whoever wants to become great must become a servant." For over seven-years God blessed me to serve all the ministry greats I have previously mention. In those seven-years I never asked for a dime. All of it was an extension of the Gift of Service that God has so graciously given me. I thank God for the opportunity to serve my Country and the FBI for over 22 1/2 years. To now, be in a position of leadership is an absolute blessing. The lessons learned by these experiences have proven valuable and I'm still serving our Perfect Will Ministries congregation, today. Thanks to everyone involved and thanks to God!

For every accomplishment, commendation, trophy, accolade, reward, recognition... I give God all the praise and honor due His name. The FBI was a huge part of my life's journey. It taught me great things and gave me great and unique experiences, but none of it could have been accomplished without God.

As I put these final words to paper, January 2015, there is a despicable thing happening in our Country right now, as it relates to Law Enforcement. Some individuals have resorted to retaliating against Police Officers for what they have perceived as injustices. All over the Country a "Vigilante" typed mentality has taken over and it is not right. Dear

God, I bind up this Spirit of Error which is a spiritual stronghold and can be found in (1 John 4:6). This scripture says: "We are from God, and whoever knows God listens to us; but whoever is not from God does not listen to us. This is how we recognize the Spirit of Truth and the Spirit of Error." God I bind up this diabolical spirit which contains contentions, false doctrines, unsubmissiveness, unteachable people, defensiveness, argumentative folk, and corruption... I bind it up in the name of Jesus and loose the Spirit of Truth, according to (Matthew 18:18), in Jesus' name. Amen!

As I spent the Christmas holiday with family in Hempstead, Long Island, NY, my attention was drawn to NYPD's Officers Wenjian Liu and Rafael Ramos. They were two Police Officers who were shot at point-blank range while sitting in their patrol car in Brooklyn, in December of 2014. Funerals for the Officers were being conducted during my stay in Hempstead. I pay homage to Officers Liu and Ramos, and their entire families. Rest in peace.

I have a parting thought for you reading this book right now. If you have not accepted Jesus Christ as your personal Savior and Lord over everything, I invite you to do it right now by repeating this simple prayer after me:

"Heavenly Father, I come to you in the Name of Jesus. I admit I'm not right with You, God. I want to be in right standing with You. I ask You to forgive me for all my sins. (Romans 10:9) says, if I declare with my mouth and believe in my heart that You raised Jesus from the dead, I would be saved. I believe it with my heart and confess it with my mouth that Jesus is my Savior and Lord over all things in my life. Come into my heart Jesus. Thank You for saving me! I pray this in Jesus' Name, Amen."

If you've prayed this for the first time, I would like to know. Please email me at, www.perfectwillministries@gmail.com or visit us at, www.perfectwillministries.com.

This message and its attachments are confidential. It may also be privileged or otherwise protected by work product doctrine or other legal guidelines. If you have received this email by mistake, please let the sender know by replying to this email; afterwards please delete this email from your computer and mail system; you may not copy this message or disclose its contents to any person, organization or entity.

CPSIA information can be obtained at www.ICGtesting.com
Printed in the USA
BVOW09s1312140515

400420BV00004B/10/P